How NOT To Be Lonely Tonight

QUOTES FROM PEOPLE WHO READ THE BOOK

"I think this book is terrific. It gave me many more ideas on how to act, to recognize the way I should have acted. I think it's fun and informative to read and will help a lot of people."

Nena, divorcée and mother
Destin, Florida

"After reading *How Not To Be Lonely Tonight*, I discovered many new places to meet the type of people I feel I can enjoy."

Don, physician
Coral Gables, Florida

"It hit *my* problem right on the button. I am exactly like one of the people mentioned in a story (I won't say which one) and I *am* going to make some adjustments."

Nathan, librarian
Fort Smith, Arkansas

"I don't really need it but I have a friend I plan to send it to. She needs to read about video dating. She's been wary of trying but it sounds like a wonderful idea."

Carol, secretary
Seabrook, Texas

"I enjoyed the book tremendously. I would recommend it to anyone."

Murray, body builder
San Antonio, Texas

"I already found my guy and I know how to keep him. We've been together just over twenty years and we are happy. However, I'm going to buy *four* books. I'll give one to my single daughter, one to my son-in-law, and two to close friends who are divorced. The book is excellent."

Patty, baseball team owner
Oklahoma City, Oklahoma

"It is a fun book and has lots of good ideas in it. I think millions of people need constant advice from people who experience the same problems as they experience and this book covers them all."

Bernard, club owner
Houston, Texas

"*How Not To Be Lonely Tonight* is real, honest and complete."

Lisa, proofreader
San Francisco

"I needed advice like this. I now take more interest in my personal appearance and plan to visit a plastic surgeon this coming week. I'm even going to a singles meeting tomorrow night and I'm anxious to try more suggestions listed in this book."

Alberta, divorced secretary
Chicago, Illinois

"Worthwhile reading. Now I understand some of the mistakes I made."

Chris, newspaper columnist
Miami, Florida

"I love it! My wife stayed up all night in order to finish it. She has several friends she will recommend it to and I have a few buddies who, I feel, need it too."

Allen, high school teacher
Metairie, Louisiana

"Candidly written. Easy to understand. And it actually works."

Brenda, social worker
New York City, New York

"*How Not To Be Lonely Tonight* can save a great many people some serious heartache. It gives us all hope."

Melanie, doctor's ex-wife
Los Angeles, California

"Thank you for your outlook and advice for us old folks. You approached our problems with respect, compassion and understanding."

Alice, widowed grandmother
Omaha, Nebraska

How NOT To Be Lonely Tonight

By Pete Billac

EAKIN PRESS ★ Austin, Texas

First Printing   October 1987
Second Printing   March 1988
Third Printing   September 1988
Fourth Printing   July 1989

Revised Edition

Copyright © 1990
By Pete Billac

Published in the United States of America
By Eakin Press
An Imprint of Eakin Publications, Inc.
P.O. Drawer 90159 ★ Austin, TX 78709-0159

ALL RIGHTS RESERVED. No part of this book may be reproduced in any form without written permission from the publisher, except for brief passages included in a review appearing in a newspaper or magazine.

ISBN 0-89015-774-X

Library of Congress Cataloging-in-Publication Data

Billac, Pete.
   [How not to be lonely]
   How not to be lonely tonight / by Pete Billac. — Rev. ed.
     p.   cm.
   Reprint. Originally published: How not to be lonely. Rev. ed. New York : Swan Publishers, 1987.
   ISBN 0-89015-774-X : $9.95 ($11.95 Can.)
   1. Loneliness. 2. Dating (Social customs) 3. Interpersonal relations. I. Title.
BF575.L7B54 1990
158'.2 — dc20
                                                             90-37148
                                                                     CIP

This book is dedicated to the millions of lonely, alone, and unhappy people in the world who are searching for companionship but haven't discovered how to find it.

And to some very special people in my life with whom I've shared some very special years. Names were omitted for a variety of obvious reasons. However, they know who they are and have my deepest thanks. I care deeply for you all.

OTHER WORKS BY THE AUTHOR:

Beneath the Gulf
The Acquiescent Wanderer
Alfredo
The Annihilator
The Last Medal of Honor

Contents

Preface		vii
What You'll Find in Each Chapter		viii
Categories of Loneliness		xiii
Chapter 1	The Physical You	1
Chapter 2	Involved With a Married Person	12
Chapter 3	They've Been Cheating On You	24
Chapter 4	Temporary Breakup	39
Chapter 5	Divorce	51
Chapter 6	How to Forget	62
Chapter 7	How to Attract a New Love	72
Chapter 8	What to Look For in a Mate	80
Chapter 9	Things You Cannot Accept	94
Chapter 10	Where to Find a New Companion	109
Chapter 11	How to Approach Someone	122
Chapter 12	Video Dating	132
Chapter 13	Let's Keep 'Em Once We Get 'Em	141
Chapter 14	Pets to Combat Loneliness	153
Chapter 15	What Do Old Folks Do?	159
A Final Note		171

Preface

Loneliness can affect both mental and physical health. It can affect your job, diet, the amount of sleep you get, and everyone and everything around you. Nights are the worst. Those hours prior to sleep can be untold torture. When you do finally fall asleep, dreams become nightmares and your heart feels as though it's going to burst wide open. That dreaded deep-down ache has engulfed your entire body and will not cease. Yes, loneliness, though not necessarily terminal, can be as painful as any agony known to mankind.

Thus the reason for this book. It tells many ways to combat loneliness and how to find happiness. It tells where to look, how to choose, and what to do in a variety of situations. It actually confronts, head-on, the problems of the majority of the lonely and alone and unhappy people in the world, then deals directly with these problems through examples, rules, and guidelines. Some chapters, interspersed with humor, will make you laugh at yourself and at how simple your problem might be to solve.

There *are* ways to end loneliness. By reading this book, you are taking the first step in working toward happiness.

What You'll Find in Each Chapter

Chapter 1 THE PHYSICAL YOU

When looking into the mirror, is there something about the "physical you" that you would like to change? Are you overweight or thin; have a large nose, small bust, or sagging jowls? If there is something physically wrong, something you feel decreases the chances of finding someone suitable, then *why not* have something done about it? A few stories, a few examples, and some solid information might lead to a decision that could change your entire romantic life.

Chapter 2 INVOLVED WITH A MARRIED PERSON

Being involved, or perhaps being in love, with someone who is married is a common occurrence in our world today. Many seem to think the "good ones" are all married. Read about one who thought so and another who just stumbled into her dilemma unknowingly. Learn how to spot a married person *before* you become close. Determine what you can do and what the pitfalls are if you remain in such a situation. Few happy endings occur when you date someone who is married. Yes, this chapter gets right to the point, with instructions and reminders of facts, some of which you may already know but would prefer to forget. Perhaps if you read about it, *this time* you'll take heed.

Chapter 3   THEY'VE BEEN CHEATING ON YOU

This happens to the majority of us. Many times, it happens more than once. Analyze what others did and thought when it happened to them. Some answers are funny; many are sad; all are poignant. This *is* a painful experience, but one you could learn to cope with through example. Become familiar with "the cheater's" profile and you'll be better equipped to spot one immediately.

Chapter 4   TEMPORARY BREAKUP

You and your companion have decided to end your present romantic involvement for a short period of time, whatever the reason. Perhaps strong feelings for each other have prevented an intelligent, satisfactory discussion of the problems. Yes, there is a change, maybe a temporary one. How should it be handled? Is there still love? Are they with someone else? Will they be back? How can you reestablish a "working relationship"? Let's work it out.

Chapter 5   DIVORCE

There are many reasons for married people to want to divorce their spouses. He could be what we might label a "model" husband, or she a "model" wife, but for one reason or another things have changed. Communication could be virtually nonexistent. The romance may have simply vanished. Both are taking each other for granted. There is no longer any excitement in once shared projects. Life is dull and changes are needed. Perhaps someone else has entered the picture. You want to live a little and feel the flame of love again. Is divorce the answer? What happens to the kids? What will happen to *you*?

Chapter 6   HOW TO FORGET

This very second there are millions of people involved in a relationship causing them unhappiness. He or she is no longer "the one" and you want to get out as quickly and painlessly as possible. It is time to *forget*! And sure, it's a bit frightening when making a big change — when changing partners after a long period of time. How to go about erasing them from your life? What to do during this adjustment period? How to handle the situation? Just what *do* you do?

Chapter 7   HOW TO ATTRACT A NEW LOVE

When someone hasn't been able to find a person to share their life, then it's time to make some adjustments within themselves. Are you boring? Laugh and smile and learn from the extroverts. Too shy? Learn to become part of the crowd. Too aggressive? Determine how to cultivate a relationship. Were you disappointed in a past romance and therefore not giving yourself a chance? When introduced, flash a big smile and make that new person feel that he or she is about to embark on a friendship with a happy, secure person. It *can* work! Learn how.

Chapter 8   WHAT TO LOOK FOR IN A MATE

There are choices to make in selecting a new mate *before* becoming involved and settling for less than what is needed to make and keep you happy. Learn how to avoid future problems when beginning a new relationship with someone new. There's a fine rundown on each prerequisite: *looks, sex, intelligence, sense of humor, security, attitude, loyalty,* and *compatibility*.

Chapter 9   THINGS YOU CANNOT ACCEPT

Warning signs in a relationship can be detected early and easily. After making your list of the positive qualities you are seeking, do not neglect to write down negative ones too. This is another reason never to rush into a relationship. Take time; be slow and smart. Discussed at length are more than a dozen *flaws* that could surely hinder and/or prevent a successful match.

Chapter 10   WHERE TO FIND A NEW COMPANION

After being one of the "alone" people and having decided to change your current status, you are ready to *hunt*. Where to begin? First, make a plan. There are so *many* places to meet the opposite sex. This, of course, depends solely on the type of person you are and the type you are searching for. In most cases, only one evening of "getting out there" can put you back "in the game." Short anecdotes exemplify the how-to's.

Chapter 11   HOW TO APPROACH SOMEONE

There are countless ways to get someone's attention without looking foolish. Every day you walk past people you'd like to meet. Or, there is someone eye-catching at the office, but it is difficult to decide what approach to take. First of all, it takes a certain amount of bravado to introduce yourself to a complete stranger. This chapter tells how *not* to "drop the ball" when a situation presents itself and how to smoothly make an approach.

Chapter 12   VIDEO DATING

There are those who scoff at the idea of video dating. However, those who have just arrived in a new town, have been recently divorced, have "ended it" with a companion, or who are just alone and lonely need all the help they can get. It's a fun, rewarding, and safe way to meet many could-be partners who might fulfill a number of "requirements." Decide how wonderful it just might be. There's no obligation. The short stories in this chapter are wild, interesting, and very true.

Chapter 13   LET'S KEEP 'EM ONCE WE GET 'EM

Having been successful in finding a new companion, you've made your various lists and practiced things to say and do to get that person. Now let's explore some methods in *keeping* them, and in helping keep the romance and the relationship alive. Communication, consideration, compromise are the three main topics of this chapter. Also included are some interesting tips on how to spoil, enjoy, and keep this partner for as long as you choose. It's easy. Just learn some tidbits of information to keep them excited and happy. And learn a few things *not* to do.

Chapter 14   PETS TO COMBAT LONELINESS

Pets aren't only for kids. Many people have a desire to be needed, and pets certainly fulfill that need. They can provide fun distractions during some "alone moments." They can be hugged, kissed, talked to, and played with. Having the responsibility of owning a pet can be a pleasant respite from problems and stress. And a walk in the park with a pet can be an excellent way to meet new people, maybe someone who shares some common interests.

Chapter 15   WHAT DO OLD FOLKS DO?

Age is truly a state of mind. Being older and alone is certainly serious, but it's a fact of life that we will all likely face some day. Suppose you have been widowed and are alone. Perhaps there's a limited income and few relatives with which to seek refuge or solace. How do you begin to ease the loneliness you feel? What can you do? There *is* a good life at seventy and eighty and even ninety. Enjoying life and having fun is not confined only to the young.

Categories of Loneliness

Being alone doesn't necessarily mean being lonely. Thousands of people are alone and not the least bit lonely. And many more are with *someone but are very lonely.*

You are either alone and lonely, or with someone and still lonely. Your loved one, for one reason or another, is either no longer around or has become disappointing. Either way, the result is unhappiness. Before a solution can be reached, the problem must first be identified. As much as we all dislike being categorized, it is necessary to pinpoint your present dilemma and offer a choice of solutions. This way, you may go directly to the chapters offering immediate relief.

CATEGORY A: One of the more common "pain-producing" categories is being in love with a person who is married — *to someone else.* You don't know how it happened, it just did. Now things must be brought to a head. Should the spouse be confronted? How about placing a *final* demand to get things rolling? Do you leave them and suffer for the remainder of your life? Or, without them, do you feel as though you no longer want to live? Chapter 2, *Involved With a Married Person,* goes directly to the heart of the matter, without fanfare and in no uncertain terms. Also, look over Chapter 6, *How to Forget,* for additional help.

CATEGORY B: You've tried — *several times* — but cannot seem to attract a suitable mate. You're either alone, lonely, or out there making all sorts of attempts, but cannot succeed. Going out with friends is nice, but — no romance. And romance is what you *want!* Do you have some physical defect that needs changing? Are you too eager? Where do you look? How do you know what's there once you've found it? If for any reason — at any age — finding the one you need seems impossible, begin with Chapter 1, *The Physical You.* Then go to Chapter 10 telling *Where to Find a New Companion,* and Chapter 12, *Video Dating,* another hunting area yet to be explored. Don't neglect *What to Look For in a Mate* in Chapter 8, or *How to Attract a New Love* in Chapter 7. Here there are answers!

CATEGORY C: Brand new discovery! Your love has been *cheating!* What to do? Leave? *Assassinate* them? Forgive them? Turn the other cheek — pretend it never happened and hope it won't happen again? If you are confused about the situation, go *directly* to Chapter 3, *They've Been Cheating.* Read about what others — men and women — did in a similar situation.

CATEGORY D: Divorce is pending. You're uncertain of the future because after *seventeen years* of marriage, all of a sudden your partner wants *out.* Is life over? Should you get a job? Live with parents? Try to reason with your mate that "things will change"? Or maybe confess personal divorce plans also to deflate their ego a bit? How about a separation? There is one chapter dedicated specifically to divorce, Chapter 5. Also read Chapter 8 on *What to Look For in a Mate,* Chapter 12, *Video Dating,* Chapter 10, *Where to Find a New Companion,* and Chapter 7, *How to Attract a New Love.*

CATEGORY E: *How to Forget* is the title of Chapter 6. Learn ways to forget the skunk once the decision to leave has been made. This is something that must be faced up to when the situation comes to the point where leaving is the *only* decision to make. Those who've made up their minds and have made the move can now find out what to do to stop their hurt.

CATEGORY F: Perhaps the loneliest of all are those in their fifties, sixties, or seventies whose loved one has just passed away. How long should mourning go on? What about remarriage? Living alone? Should one live with the kids or go to an old folks home? There are myriad options. Most of all, keep that desire to go on living and to *not* be lonely. Chapter 15, *What Do Old Folks Do?*, is dedicated to those of you who act or feel "old." However, many of the other chapters apply also. You might be older, but your life is not over; maybe it's just a new beginning!

Chapter One

The Physical You

Having been forewarned in the preface that this book will bear a certain amount of humor, don't be surprised when the first chapter seems to have a preponderance of "descriptive laughables." Nevertheless, answers are here for those who have placed themselves in this category. Make a choice soon whether to do something about being lonely, or whether to stay lonely.

Not everyone has been "blessed by the gods" with a super physical appearance. Perhaps large ears are a problem, or maybe people can't tell whether that's your nose or a banana you're eating. Being too thin — or too fat — can seem awful, as can thinning hair or a small bust. Premature wrinkles, being too short or too tall, also can be problems. The truth of the matter is that it is *all up to you* to alter your life and make it a more fulfilling one.

FAT OR THIN?

Happy fat? Then *stay* fat! Think it's chic to be bone thin and bustless? Then *stay* thin! Have a feeling that muscles repel women? Then keep those straight, skinny arms. But if there is *anything* about your physical appearance causing you to feel companionship or romance might bypass you, the *only* way to change is to *do something about it!*

Let's say you're overweight, not a member of one of those "Big is Beautiful" clubs, and truly want to lose those excess pounds to look and feel better. Again, it's up to *you!* There are countless diets on the market. Most of them will aid in shedding pounds, but when it comes down to the nitty-gritty, *discipline* is the answer. Eat the *right* foods and don't pig out on the *wrong* ones. And make a habit of it. If you're not hungry, why eat? If you're full and there is still food on your plate, stop eating.

Yes, it's that simple. I do not recommend a crash diet. It might have taken years to add on that blubber. Then how in the world can results be seen and felt immediately? The best program is a sensible exercise program and a change of eating habits.

Low on discipline? Try joining a health club and let them provide the motivation needed to become the thin person you would like to see in the mirror. If, after several months, you feel you need more profound measures to completely reach your goal, then it might be time to seek the advice of a plastic surgeon. *Liposuction* is a new procedure for extracting fat with a gadget while the patient sits and watches it disappear. The cost varies with the amount of fat and the areas from which it is to be removed. Plan on spending $3,000 up!

Those with an underweight problem should reverse the procedure. Try weight training. There are foods that aid in gaining (just talk to the fat person) and you *can* get heavier. Don't expect a miracle, but *do* expect a vast improvement through some weight gain and muscle toning. A thin person with definition looks great! The very *last* thing people who are unhappy with their weight should do is *nothing*, then wallow in self-pity. Do something positive! Then go out and find someone who appreciates you. *Do* it and be *seen!*

NOT TO BE NOSY, OR ANYTHING . . .

If it hampers your chances of *not* being lonely, correct it. How about a large nose or one that is humped or "eagle beaked"? We've all seen them. Sometimes it is simply amazing what a profound change can take place once this problem is remedied.

One very intimate experience was one I shared with my girlfriend. I thought she was gorgeous, but a bump on her nose caused her to feel she must only face people straight on. She hadn't had a side-view picture taken since she was preteen. We visited a plastic surgeon and he told her what to expect. The cost was $2,500 and the operation was handled in an outpatient clinic with local anesthesia. It took about thirty minutes. In fact, during surgery, a mirror was brought in so she could see what was taking place. She felt no pain.

After the operation, I drove her back to her apartment. Her face was bandaged. The following morning her eyes were swollen and discolored, and she had a slight nosebleed. Still, no pain! Within ten days the swelling and discoloration had almost vanished. She proudly showed her new nose to her friends and family, turning to the side for the first time in fifteen long, hump-nosed years. I thought she was terrific-looking before, but *now*, she is movie-star glamorous. The change was fantastic, and she recommends it for everyone.

If I had a nose that made me feel self-conscious, I'd do something about it. I'd earn the money, save it, or borrow it. If worse came to worse, I might even consider robbing parking meters. At least upon release from prison, I'd have a nice nose to face the world — head on *or* from the side!

"FIGURATIVELY" SPEAKING

Let's suppose you're tired of wearing a sweater with beestings showing where your bust should be. Or maybe you have oversized or sagging breasts. Why *not* have this remedied by a plastic surgeon? If you feel your sweater would be more appealing to others and more personally satisfying with mounds — then, for cryin' out loud, *get* those mounds! I said "mounds," now, not *mountains*!

I interviewed over 400 women who have undergone bust enlargement, and each one was pleased. A few of the greedy had to go back to have a little size reduction and settled for a respectable "pair." One shouldn't be concerned about the firmness. They look and feel *sooo* real! Numbness (as some say there is) tends to disappear within a short period of time.

Many years ago, when the first bust implants were tested, I was on an elevator in a doctor's clinic where a woman brushed against me. I threw my arms up in the air, thinking I was being robbed by a gunman with two pistols! Yes, the first type were as hard as rocks. Still, the people I interviewed (some with the hard kind) preferred rocks to flatland.

See a plastic surgeon to discuss any breast size problems. The consultation might cost you fifty bucks, but it's worth it. Learn about various procedures as well as glance over a boob "mug" book on happy former patients. *Then* make up your mind. Expect to pay about $1,500 up.

HAIR TODAY... GONE TOMORROW?

Now, on to the men about baldness. If you have lost or are losing hair, and some magic potion hasn't come out since I've written this book, why not do something about it? You can get transplants, weaves, partial toupees, or the full kind you slip on like a lady's swimming cap. The various surgical techniques can be explained by a doctor, or watch that guy on

TV who talks about wearing a hairpiece. Send for his free booklet.

Too often men wear toupees that are highly obvious. Either they have lost their vanity or are just lazy, making a half-hearted attempt to improve themselves. With "real hair," the hairpiece is ordered to look exactly like your own. A skull measurement is taken, and the actual hair color is matched to your satisfaction. Weeks later, it arrives and is cut and shaped to bring out a new you.

There are expensive models and there are bad models. Real hair toupees begin at about $1,000 and may go on up according to personal affordability and how much rent the hairdresser needs to pay. They look and feel better than the synthetic kind, but need regular maintenance. Real hair tends to discolor in the sun and needs attention. Many well-known movie stars sport hairpieces and they look terrific. Yours can look as good as theirs for a fraction of the cost.

Synthetic hair looks *almost* like the real stuff, and you are measured and color-matched in the same way. It absolutely never discolors and lasts several years, from one to three in many instances, with periodic maintenance. If you can afford it, why not have one of each: synthetic for play and bumming around, and the real stuff for special outings.

Choices for attaching your toupee are clips or tape. Clips are easier to attach, but tape fits more snugly.

Whichever you choose, take a little time while grooming. If the "rug" is on crooked, or you don't comb it correctly, then it becomes noticeable. Otherwise, only your hairdresser and your best friends know. Don't be self-conscious about it. Whatever kind you choose, it must look better than nothing or hair combed all the way across your head, from ear to ear, to stop the glare.

One thing the ads say is that "you can swim with it." Sure you can. Just don't get your head *under* the water, because I've seen men who did emerge from the pool looking as if a rat had died on their head. One fellow finished a tough tennis match and his head looked like a porcupine during mating season. Make allowances to keep your beauty under control. Wear a hat, cap, or headband. If swimming underwater, wear a bathing cap. For tennis, wear a hat, then wipe with a towel. Then keep that towel on your head until you get in the clubhouse or maybe the sanctity of a pay toilet. While riding in convertibles, *do* wear a cap and cram it down almost to ear level. I once saw a hairpiece fly through the air on a freeway. The driver who lost it, several cars ahead, almost caused a ten-car collision. Hair spray will keep it neat in a mild wind, but for any breeze stronger than that of a ten-buck fan, wear something.

Hairdressers (with kindness) refer to hairpieces as "units." I advise two units for safety, since they all need maintenance and you'll need an extra while one is being redyed or having hair replaced. If you are going to opt for this method of hair replacement, do it the correct way. Take as much time with this "new" hair as you did before the loss. Make it look real. That's the object of hair replacement, isn't it? And if you don't like the way it looks, tell them about it and have them correct it!

The synthetic models begin at about $300 and go up. Usually, a good one is about $500 plus. Go to a few places that sell hairpieces before making up your mind. Examine their "toup" book and decide which model and price suits you. A good toupee will make you look and feel years younger and will definitely make you more attractive.

PLASTIC SURGERY — IS IT WORTH IT?

Plastic surgery is *wonderful*! Did you know you can be made taller or shorter by plastic surgery? Wrinkles can be removed, tummy flattened, face sanded, and many other things made smaller or harder? It has made many so happy. If it's affordable, I say *do it*! Anything that will aid in preventing loneliness should be done without looking back.

I deliberated several weeks before deciding to put this next bit of corrective surgery into this book, but it is well worth the effort on my part, and certainly, the effort and investment on your part, if this happens to be your problem area. It is called the *penile prosthesis*. I promise to give this information in layman's terms. To do so might sound a bit silly, but here goes.

Impotency is an ugly word to men, perhaps *the* ugliest word in the dictionary. But there is something you can do about it surgically. There are two basic types of penile prosthesis: the inflatable and the non-inflatable. The non-inflatable consists of two sponge-filled silicone rods with no movable parts. They are inserted in the sides of the penis and provide sufficient length, width, and girth to stimulate the normal erectile response. It makes the organ rigid enough to insert inside the vaginal canal. (Yes, it will end the dilemma of "trying to force a raw oyster into a slot machine.") It can penetrate and move in and out with normal feeling and normal results, enabling one to reach ejaculation. The main disadvantage is that the penis remains in a state of semi-erection, and one might need super-strength underwear to keep from being obvious.

The inflatable kind consists of a hollow silicone cylinder placed along the sides of your penis. A reservoir containing radiopaque solution is sutured into the abdominal facia, and a bulb is implanted in one scrotal sac. The cylinders, reservoir, and bulb are connected by silicone tubes. When you squeeze your "ball bulb," the solution flows from the reservoir to the cylinders implanted in the sides of your penis. The cylinders, when filled with this solution, strengthen and *presto!* "UP" you are! A one-way check valve in the pump keeps the cylinders filled with fluid to stay "up" for as long as you choose. When you no longer want an erection, simply compress a release valve located in the lower portion of the bulb in the scrotum. This causes the fluid to return to the reservoir, and you return to a relaxed position.

There is hardly a more helpless feeling known to mankind than that of a man who cannot "get it up" when the situation presents itself. It has happened to most males over the age of thirty who have had sexual contact with another person. There are several thousand penile prosthesis operations going on each day in the United States alone. After determining it isn't job worries, going out with your best friend's wife, financial problems, fear of trying to *perform* with incredible fervor so she will never forget you — and after you've consulted your best friend, your therapist, and prayed a lot — perhaps an operation is all that is left.

This just might be *the* answer to your problem. It's easy to see the advantage of having this inflatable penile prosthesis as a permanent cure to organic impotence. "Get it up" as often as desired, and for as long as desired, with just a little squeeze. Pretend you are fumbling with your zipper or giving yourself one of those satisfying scratches baseball players always seem to be doing, and you're ready to please *everybody*! The cost is in the $3,000 range and up.

See how *fantastic* modern science is? Look how far we've come in the past few decades. This operation has saved many marriages and relationships from being shattered. It has returned an active sex life to men who needed it to live a life worth living. Fortunate are you who can scoff at any of this, those who will never need an operation of any kind, much less one of this magnitude. But to those of you who do, thank the Lord and medical science for the opportunity.

Now, let's go on to the face lift. On this subject there are so many questions many are afraid to ask, questions that need answers. I hope that my brief discussion might give the necessary nudge prompting a visit to a plastic surgeon who has all the answers.

Unlike operations on the nose and bust, the face lift does

not last forever. It depends on the individual: on age, weight, and the amount of elasticity in the skin. A face lift is a certain, immediate way to look and feel years younger. Methods of lifting include placing silicone under the skin to push the wrinkles out, or by surgically cutting and stretching the skin.

The medical term for face lift is *rhytidectomy*, from the Greek word for *wrinkle*. Basically, the face lift removes saggy skin, thereby eliminating heavy folds under the cheeks and jowls. An incision begins at the hairline or temple region, goes downward in front of the ear, around the earlobe, into the hairline of the scalp, and continues within the hairline to the back of the scalp. It makes the recipient feel and look years younger.

Many famous people admit to face lifts. Many more do not. Again, I think it's a wonderful idea. If you can afford it, go visit that plastic surgeon for more information, pictures, and costs.

Men are less likely to take advantage of a face lift because the operation does leave a scar that, in women, is hidden in the hairline. It is not as easy to hide in men. In some men, a skilled surgeon can take advantage of whatever "character lines" they might have. (Notice I did not say "wrinkles" in describing the men. Just another unfairness that women, alone, have to bear.)

On the dark side, I have seen some who have had several lifts, and you'd swear they have been victims of Jivaros. One lady who admitted to having three operations had the problem that when she raised her eyebrows, her mouth opened!

Having a face lift is an individual thing — a personal decision. If you feel loneliness or unhappiness is caused by the fear of getting or looking old, then do something about it. Yes, if the lack of certain attributes is keeping you from finding that wonderful person in your life — and it very well could be — do your damnedest to correct it through plastic surgery, once all other means have been exhausted.

CAN A SIMPLE SOLUTION HELP?

If it's a minor correction, a hairdresser or beauty consultant can do wonders ... perhaps a new hairstyle, new blush, some color added to the eyelids, or a different lipstick. Maybe exercise will remove that double chin or a different style of clothes will change your image. When these means have not satisfied you, *then* go for surgery. The cost depends on what needs to be done and on what your physician charges.

If it will make you happy and *not* lonely, go for it with gusto! There's a wonderful world out there and we are meant to be happy and share things with others. At least learn about your options. In the end, it all comes down to that one person —*you!*

The way we look is important. From my five-year survey of over 6,000 people across the United States, the following are the three top "wants" a man looks for in a woman.

(1) A man wants a woman to be *attractive*. He can look like a warthog, makes no difference. He wants the lady to look good.
(2) Men *demand* loyalty. They want to be able to trust their partner under any circumstances.
(3) Men want *compatibility*! By "compatibility" most men mean they can hunt, fish, play golf, or watch TV all weekend without their wife/girlfriend complaining too much.

Men always notice the way a woman looks. No matter how unfair this may seem, it is reality.

Now, what did my survey show a woman wanted mostly in a man? The top three things were . . .

(1) A woman wants a man to have a *sense of humor*. Respondents didn't look for the most handsome man. Oh, they didn't want him to ring the bells at Notre Dame, but they preferred personality over looks.
(2) A woman would *like* loyalty. Yes, women want their men to be honest and true to them.
(3) They want that sucker to *have a job*!

No hairy chest, well-shaped butt, tall and lean preferences. No! Women wanted the above things. And when you think about it, it makes a lot of sense, doesn't it?

Chapter Two

Involved With a Married Person

This heads the list in the loneliness department. It truly is a no-win situation, but it's happening this very moment to thousands of people all over the world. Those of you in this situation already know just about everything written here. Let's hope that *this* time, you'll follow one of the solutions to get your life back on track.

The reasons *not* to be involved with a married person far outnumber the reasons *to* be involved. Not often is the answer easy, or the problem a matter of black or white. Oftentimes there are gray areas, and here is where it pays to be smart, and maybe a little brave. You must prepare yourself to face disappointment.

When there's a "gray area" problem, that is, when you can't decide whether you should or shouldn't, compose a list of the good and not-so-good things about the person. It is necessary to be truthful with pros and cons, or you'll only continue kidding yourself and will probably stay on the road that surely will lead to disaster. Once you make this list, take a hard look at what the future might be with this relationship, if any. Remember, we're discussing *your* life, *your* happiness, *your* future. We're talking about how *not* to be lonely. If you are unfortunately already in love with someone married, prepare yourself for *many* days and nights of loneliness.

There are extenuating circumstances in some of these married person-dating-a-single person romances, but let's discuss the overwhelming amount of information we have concerning such relationships.

The quickest answer is to *avoid* anyone who is married. It is not true the "best are already taken." There are thousands and thousands of people out there, unmarried and eligible, who are also searching for someone. Later in this book we'll discuss where they are, how to find them, and what to expect from them.

Yes, try to avoid a relationship with someone who is married. If you are already involved, here is the best solution: *get the hell out of it* as quickly as possible! Do not hesitate. Do not pass go. Get out now and try *never* to look back. Be prepared to face some lonely times — for a while, to suffer a little. I promise this little bit of hurting and suffering now will be far less than the hurt and suffering you will have to endure later.

Before we discuss how to get out of the situation, let's review some short, real-life stories of a few who have fallen into the trap. Chances are that one of these is similar to your present dilemma.

EXAMPLE 1:

Judy, age twenty-four, is a secretary in a large public relations office. She sees all sorts of men coming and going, traveling salesmen as well as some of the executives in her own company. Trouble is, most of them are married. And the married "players" somehow manage to keep their marital status a secret.

One day, Ron, who is thirty-five and a new man with the company, invited Judy to lunch. He wasn't wearing a wedding ring; he was attractive, seemed nice, and Judy was hungry. Judy didn't feel like coming right out and asking whether he was married because Ron seemed more single than many of the other men in her office whom she knew were single. When Ron asked her to go sailing with him that coming weekend, Judy was certain he was single. "Surely if he was married," Judy reasoned, "he wouldn't have the weekend off to spend with me."

Wrong, Judy! The guy works for a public relations firm. He makes many trips on weekends and nights during the week. Too, married players are oftentimes more smooth than single ones. The single guys can go through their "hit and miss" tactics over and over again and let the law of averages prevail. Married men, on the other hand, have limited time. They must intelligently seek out their prey and pounce on it quickly. They must be experienced and *lethal*, as their time is more limited. Ron was a perfect example.

Well, Judy went sailing with Ron that Saturday, and they spent that evening on the boat. When Sunday came around, Judy was "involved" with a married man! It was the beginning of her trouble. Of course, she could have asked if he was married, but she didn't want to sound too sophomorish, and she wanted him *not* to be married. The "wanting" has no bearing whatsoever on reality. He *is* married and Judy is heading for heartbreak to add to her loneliness.

Ron called her a few times the following week, took her to lunch once, dinner twice, and had two "sessions" in her apartment — *her* apartment! And, believe it or not, he came up with the story about having a roommate who was in residency at the local hospital and — *Judy went for it!* Their alliance went on for a few months. Then Ron couldn't be with Judy on his birthday. Of course not! He had to be with his wife and two kids on that special occasion. He made a "business" excuse to Judy.

The Christmas season was approaching and Ron took Judy to the office party. He just didn't happen to mention the party to his wife. But on Christmas Eve, Ron was tucked away safely at home with his family. Judy, of course, was at home also — but *alone*. The telephone number he had given her to call, the one she was to call *only* in an emergency, was not a working number. Judy didn't know what to do. She waited patiently by the telephone, but to no avail. Sleep was not about to happen. During a night of tossing and turning, her subconscious was listening for that heart-mending phone call. Her conscious mind was telling her he hadn't been in an accident; he wasn't doing business. He was with someone else, probably his wife. There could be no other explanation.

When morning came, Judy looked awful. This was her first evening of suffering. Christmas Day and night she was in agony. What she did then determined how many additional evenings she would spend like the last two. The following day she arrived at work the second the guard opened the doors to the building. She was a complete wreck. Judy *knew* Ron would have an excuse, but she also knew there *was* no excuse she could possibly accept. She knew, *now* in her heart, the one thing she was afraid to ask was a reality. Judy realized that all her "wanting him not to be married" was in vain.

Ron came through the door with the usual wide grin on his face, prepared. He knew, from past similar experiences, an explanation was needed. Being crafty, he was practiced in deceit. Ron was one of the married, *professional* cheaters. Judy could hardly contain herself. The rest of the office force within the immediate area sensed a storm was brewing. Ron was a top executive. Only his boss was acquainted with his marital status. Ron walked up to Judy's desk and pulled a bouquet of flowers from behind his back. "I can explain, hon," he told her. "Just know that I love you and I missed you and that, at lunch, I'll explain it all."

Those next few hours were pure hell for Judy. What

Involved With a Married Person

could he explain? He'd left her at home on *Christmas Eve*, his telephone was not a working number, and he never called. What could he *possibly* have been doing that any excuse would pardon? At lunch, Ron, head lowered, Judy's hand in his, even a tear escaping from one eye, told her that he was married. Judy had prepared herself for his confession. At least, she thought she had.

Judy rose from the table, picked up her purse, turned and left. She called work to report that she was sick and went back to her apartment, locked the door, took the phone off the hook, and cried herself to sleep. She was devastated! She had strong feelings for Ron — maybe even love. He was charming, attentive, and with her much of the time. And Ron cared for Judy. But he cared for his wife and kids also, and when it came to a choice, Judy would have to take a hike. It was that simple. Judy was the minority stockholder in this corporation, as are the majority of the women who are dating married men.

What does Judy do? She feels betrayed. She also feels stupid. She had suspicions, but was too weak to ask for, and not that willing to accept, an answer. What does she do now? Her life feels as though it has ended. She could accept the role of playing "second fiddle" and allow the relationship to continue as Ron suggested when she exited from their luncheon meeting. Naturally, Ron would suggest that. He's a cheater, remember?

If Judy does accept a part-time relationship with Ron, what is to be her future? She'll always have to accept those hurried, hushed phone calls while he's on vacation with his family. On those special days — *Christmas, New Year's Eve, Valentine's Day* and on and on — she will have to understand that those days will be spent alone *and* lonely! She can never plan on a family of her own, either. He already has one. She'll also have to continue meeting in those quaint little out-of-the-way places she thought were so romantic before she learned they were necessary. She can never have someone to call her very own. When she truly needs him, chances are he cannot be there. When he needs her, someone else — *his wife* — is there to help.

The simple solution is the one we all know must be made eventually. It is *over*! It has *ended*! Judy must *get out*! Just remember, no matter how severe the hurt seems now, it will soon pass. The alternative of staying involved is not a choice — it's a *sentence*!

Judy got out. Within a few months, she met someone new. He has been her special someone for almost three years. BUT — he, too, is *married*! Won't Judy ever learn? Yes, she has. That special someone is married — to JUDY! See, life doesn't end because you were involved with a married person, but it certainly can be total misery if you *remain* in that situation.

LOOK FOR SIGNS

Now, some tips on what to look for so you can avoid beginning a relationship with one of these "untouchables." Other than a ring, there might be a ring *mark*! If he doesn't ask you to *his* apartment on at least the second or third date, make certain you hold onto your feelings and put him in the "suspect" category. Don't go for those lame reasons about "a roommate who is studying" or is "on a swing-shift." Don't be so gullible about these things. That is how many of you got into this predicament in the first place. You went in blindly, eyes *and* brains closed.

If he takes you to these little off-the-beaten-path places *all* the time, he could be an incurable romantic or short of funds. *Or* he could be hiding from eyes that might spill the beans to his wife. If he is hurried most of the time and is not an obstetrician who makes house calls or an ambulance driver, be suspicious. If, during a phone conversation, he has to hang up quickly, suspect that, too. If his parents live in town, you've

Involved With a Married Person

been dating a few months, and he still hasn't shown you off, face the fact that he either thinks you're unattractive, common, or he already *has* someone who knows his parents.

There *are* signs. Any nincompoop can find them if he'll just look. Don't kid yourself and not want there to be any telltale evidence. So *what* if you find out he's married? Better to find out now and waste moments, as compared to wasting months or years in a no-win situation.

EXAMPLE 2:

Cathy, almost thirty, has two children ages eight and ten and has been divorced five years. She's had a few relationships since her divorce, but all were disappointing. "Men always seem to be looking for only one thing. When they find out I'm divorced, they all seem to think I'm just looking for sex. None of them want responsibility or commitment, and most are not fond of the idea of having to raise 'another man's family'!" Cathy is a nurse at a local hospital. Most of the doctors, she's found, are already married.

Many of these doctors have wives who worked to put them through medical school, and maybe even supported a child or two. Now the doctor has established his practice and is feeling that his many years of sacrificing and study have earned him the *right* to play. And what about his wife? When is it *her* turn to play? Hasn't *she* earned something also?

She has spent the last ten years working. She worked in the bookstore during school so hubby could have time alone, undisturbed, to study. When that first lump appeared in her stomach, she had to halt her own education, still work part-time, have the baby, then go to work full-time. Then, when that *second* lump came upon the scene and was growing each day, thumping at night to get out of that dark place, she had to sleep on the sofa so as not to disturb *his* rest. She was bringing home the money, keeping house, and cooking too. She spent several years after the birth of the two babies wiping snot from their noses, staying up with them at night when they were sick, and changing crappy diapers. When in the hell is *her* time to have fun?

Cathy, of course, never once considered that side of the coin. She was concerned *only* for her own welfare. She had two kids who were getting too old to accept the fact that "uncles" visited so often. Sometimes they stayed overnight or for a few days. Sometimes they came over periodically for a month or so, then just disappeared, never to be mentioned again.

Cathy decided that she would become a mistress. Why not spend an afternoon, a night, or a weekend now and then with a married doctor who was established and could afford *two* households? It would be a lot better than waiting tables at that greasy neighborhood restaurant for an additional hundred bucks a week. She could spend more time with the kids, not chance losing their respect with those visiting uncles, and live easy for a while. A permanent companionship could come later on; maybe when the kids were grown. Cathy went after the forty-two-year-old hospital administrator, the one who felt he deserved some extracurricular frivolity and could now afford it.

Within a few weeks Cathy had her "situation." She quit her three-nights-a-week job and spent some of those nights with her new sponsor. Sometimes she traveled over long weekends to some exciting places, and that extra money he bestowed on her for her favors helped her own troubled financial situation. Cathy had her children, more money, and a lover who allowed her freedom. Well, not absolute freedom, you understand. Naw, the bastard *demanded* loyalty from Cathy. If he even suspected she was seeing someone else, he would cut off her money supply and their little peccadillo would be ended.

This affair between Cathy and the administrator went on for almost three years. Then, it all came to a screeching halt. Wifey became suspicious when her philanderer/husband spent too much time on so-called emergency hospital calls. She decided she would follow him one evening. She watched as he met Cathy at this little restaurant and waited outside while they had dinner, then watched as they drove to the hideaway apartment he and two married doctors rented as their "home away from home" playpen. The wife waited in the car as the rain began to fall. Her insides turned sour. She was in torment. All the years of struggling and caring for this man, all the sacrifices she'd made, all the living given up for him — for their family — were now down the tube because some cheap little hussy threw herself at him. She followed them back to the restaurant, taking down the license plate number of Cathy's car. Soon that would tell everything.

Let's see how this situation affected all three.

The Wife: She couldn't decide which course to take but finally went home, not mentioning it to her husband, and thought things over. She became depressed. Every time hubby was late getting home, the "other woman" was suspected. In the following weeks the wife became tearful and began drinking a little too much, trying to erase the pain. She began calling Cathy and hanging up. There were feelings of confusion and suffering. This man she had worked for and loved for so many years, the father of her children, was now involved with someone else. All sorts of mental pictures of them "doing things" together floated before her eyes.

The wife sought the advice of her best friend. There were few options. Among them: divorce the guy and leave him with only the clothes on his back, or perhaps confront him with the situation and make him swear never to do it again. She could accept it and *pretend* nothing had happened while seeking a part-time life of her own. Divorce wasn't really a solution. What possibilities were there? Going back to work would be difficult — nearly impossible — with the children not fully grown, even with the settlement and alimony. The diaper-washing, nose-wiping days were over. She had a beautiful house, fine furniture, large swimming pool, a new Cadillac in the garage, and enjoyed playing golf three days a week at the country club.

Finally, she decided to talk it out with her husband, inform him she knew of his philandering and if he didn't stop, she would leave him in abject poverty. The bluff worked. Hoping he'll keep his pants zipped when he's away from home other than to take a leak, she has decided to stick it out with him.

The Husband: He has confessed all, admitting he "tried" to have an affair with that flirty little nurse — *three* times — but could not perform the dastardly deed either "out of love for his wife" or "from feeling guilty over cheating on her." He apologized profusely and swore on all that was sacred to him never to do it again. After begging forgiveness, he decided his best defense was a strong offense. Yep, if she, his wife, had not spent so much time at the country club, had paid more attention to him, and taken a more active interest in his career, he never would have fallen prey to a seductress. The smart bastard convinced his wife it was all her fault. After a few months of "playing it cool," the guy was at it again, accepting the attentions of another nurse, and having a similar affair as the one with Cathy.

Cathy: Having conditioned herself to accept the fact that, one day, it would be over, Cathy felt little except the loss of some easy money. Since her "meal-ticket's" wife found out about the affair she, of course, had to seek employment elsewhere. No problem about getting a good recommendation. She could have taken her job back as a waitress a few nights per week, maybe expose the kids to a few additional uncles until she made a more permanent connection, but Cathy is a survivor. Within a few weeks Cathy had another "alliance" with a married doctor, and so the saga of "Mistress Cathy" continues.

Quite an ending, huh? Think it worked out for all con-

Involved With a Married Person

cerned? It hasn't. The wife is in torment. Her dreams torture her and most of the time, she cannot sleep until complete exhaustion forces her to. Every night her husband is away, she has visions of him cheating with someone else, whether he's on legitimate business or not. Her unhappiness means that, although she is not alone, she's very lonely. After considering having an affair of her own, her distrust of men prevented it. Few hear her laugh very much anymore, but they do hear her snap at the kids. She's lost interest in being healthy, drinks more than before, and has a figure filling out in all the wrong places. She is not the same person she was prior to her sad discovery.

Cathy is about eight years older now and has lost most of the respect her two children had for her, and pretty much lost total respect for herself. She's been through four married doctors and has had to change hospitals twice. This has resulted in even more conniving and callous ways than before. Playing the role of mistress/prostitute/mother has a way of hardening a person. She might have had a better chance at slinging hash those three nights and, sooner or later, a nice guy would have come along assuring that her world would *not* be a lonely one. When the kids grow up and leave, where will Cathy be then?

The husband thinks he came out ahead. His new mistress is younger than Cathy. He is almost fifty. His wife looks awful and they haven't "slept" together in a few years. But she keeps busy and stays out of his way, and that seems to be all he cares about. He has his career and a well-paid relationship and doesn't bother to conceal his philandering in the presence of mutual friends. Sometimes, though, he wonders where it will end. Several times he happened to see his mistress with one of the younger doctors having lunch and wondered if she might be searching for someone new, someone younger. Even with financial success, happiness is elusive. He's aware that he is being used in his extramarital relationship just as he is using his mistress. Many nights, while at home in his own bed alone, he wonders if his life should have — could have — taken a different route causing contentment. Where will he be ten years from today and even ten more years from then? Is it worth it?

I could relate story after story, but they all follow the same basic scenario, and most have the same ending: several people are hurt and several lives are devastated.

GETTING OUT

So you are involved with a married person. What can you do? Take the advice of a friend who was against this from the start. They won't tell you much other than "get out of it," but they've been telling you that all along, haven't they? A talk with your church minister might help, although it would be embarrassing to admit what you've been doing. The minister will probably offer to pray for you, tell you it's a sin, and advise you to get out of it. A psychiatrist or psychologist can explain why you are in that situation, but you know why you're in it. If you just want *out* as painlessly as possible, these sources can give you further insight on how to accomplish that.

After you've tried the various outlets I've suggested, be prepared to hurt a little. Perhaps you care for this person and you'll spend some sleepless nights wracked with pain and loneliness. It's normal. Hopefully, some of these suggestions can cut this mourning time to a minimum and give peace of mind.

When it is over with "them," you'll be on your way to seeking happiness and contentment. Go out and search for someone who can fulfill your needs and be available to share his/her life with you. Get out of that sick situation. Happiness is out there for anyone who will reach for it and give it a chance. *You* — be that someone!

Chapter Three

They've Been Cheating On You

Interviews and comments from the ones "wronged" will begin this chapter, giving a variety of viewpoints from which to identify. Yes, before "throwing the bum out," or "shooting him below the belt" or "crying a flood of tears," explore the feelings of others in a similar situation. It seems, too, that men are the usual culprits in these "straying efforts," but know that in this world of more "freedom," women also are fast approaching a sizable percentage. Recent statistics say seventy-four percent of married men and fifty percent of married women have cheated on their mates in marriages lasting five years or longer. Nevertheless, *someone* has strayed, so let's talk to the women first.

The majority of these interviews were taken in large cities such as Miami, New Orleans, Houston, Oklahoma City, Chicago, New York City, Cleveland, Des Moines, Spokane, Los Angeles, Las Vegas, Albuquerque, Dallas, and Kansas City. Interviews from small towns are included also, from such spots as Pea Ridge, Arkansas; Livingston, Texas; Muskogee,

Oklahoma; Needles, Arizona; Salinas, California; Excelsior Springs, Kansas; and Stonewall, Mississippi.

"My boyfriend, when I was twenty, was truly wonderful in every way. Upon discovering a letter hidden in his sock drawer, I was hurt. I cried, pouted, stormed out of his apartment, brushing him aside. At home there came more tears. He found the letter I'd torn up and called. I hung up and wouldn't talk to him for days, but I missed him. Within a week we were back together again, but something was missing. My trust in him was gone and a permanent relationship was impossible. We dated a few more months and then just drifted apart."

Lauren, twenty-six, a schoolteacher

"When a friend told me my husband was having an affair with his secretary, I felt all sick inside. The very thought of him being 'with' someone else — close and touching — made me ill. We had three kids during our thirteen-year marriage. Now I wondered what he was doing, how many times, was she the first? Every thought made me hurt. I considered divorce, then thought how it would affect the children and me. I wasn't angry, just empty inside. When confronted with the facts, he admitted it and there was shame on his face. He vowed never to see her again. I went for his 'I don't know why I did it routine,' but keep steady tabs on him. Three years have passed and, if he is still seeing someone, he's got to be the 'fastest gun in the west.' He must check in with me almost every hour. How long this will continue, I don't know, but it has made life miserable for both of us. What to do . . . just try and forget it, I guess."

Stephanie, thirty-six, housewife

"It hasn't happened to me yet, but if it did, my first move would be to write my boyfriend a long letter explaining my feelings on trust and my reluctance to date someone who had promised to be faithful, then wasn't. I'd put him 'through the mill' and hope the jerk suffered. And, if he left for good, I'd just have to shrug my shoulders and feel that I was better off without him."

Cynthia, twenty-two, secretary

"If I found my guy cheating on me, I'd blow the bastard's *balls* off."

Velma, thirty-one, truck-stop waitress

"My husband and I grew up together. We were in grade school, high school and, when I quit college to put him through medical school, I didn't mind the sacrifice at all. Everything was going well. We still made love as frequently as most, he was a good father and a thoughtful husband. When his mistress phoned to tell me she was *pregnant* and to give him a divorce, at first I thought it was a morbid joke. Finding out it was true, I casually confronted him with it after dinner when the kids were in bed. He almost fainted. At first he denied it and, when I suggested we go talk to the caller (she gave me her name, address, phone number, and I wondered if her social security number would be next), he admitted it. He couldn't explain why, but vowed to *try* to stop. I asked him to leave and pick up his things in the morning. I went to an attorney, got a divorce, good alimony and child support settlements, and went out to find someone new. I'd have been willing to give him a chance to discontinue his antics and would have consented to staying with him, knowing deep in my heart that something had been taken away that couldn't be regained — *trust*. My present marriage to a fine man who left a cheating wife is a deliriously happy one."

Kathi, forty-five, housewife and golfer

"The very first thing I did upon finding out, when I *saw*

him kiss a girl good-bye at a popular luncheon spot, was go back to the apartment, pack my things, and go to Mother's! I cried for one week, got angry the following weeks and then went back to watch him squirm. The idea of getting 'caught in the act' scared the hell out of him, at least, I hope so. He has been attentive, apologetic, gave me an excuse I'd like to believe, and I am trying to trust him again. It's been about six months since that fateful afternoon and we are still together. Yes, a little bit of trust is missing, but he treats me so fine now, that I'm giving him the benefit of the doubt."

Angela, twenty-seven, legal secretary

"This guy had *nerve!* He actually *told* me he was 'thinking' of having an affair with a waitress. He said she was beautiful and sweet and was interested in what he had to say. *Hmmm*, I thought. *Maybe he's trying to tell me something.* I told him to please think it over, that if he did deceive me, I'd leave. I began to really listen to him, asked him about his work, his wants and pet peeves about me. It's surprisingly wonderful, if two people use their power of reasoning, how well things can work out. He hasn't mentioned the waitress in many months. We have both made a few changes and are so much happier with each other."

Mary, thirty-one, clinical psychologist

"If that -*!*?! cheated on me, he'd regret it for the rest of his life. I'd go to bed with his best friend and as many other of his friends as possible. I know, I *know!* It might not make things better and, in fact, could hurt me more, but I'd do it anyway."

Tanya, twenty-six, airline stewardess

"I guess I'd go out, get drunk, and hope it was just a bad dream. I'm sort of weak and would probably ask him about it. And if he told me something sensible, I'd forgive him. Caring for him so much makes it hard to imagine being with anyone else. Hopefully, he'll never stray. I love him with all my heart."

Leah, twenty-four, salesperson

"If I found out he was cheating, I'd have to ask him why and try to find out what went wrong. My dad cheated on my mom and they stayed together, unhappily, for years after. Of course I'd cry and feel hurt, wanting an answer — then decide what to do from there. If he vowed never to do it again, I'd feel better. But eventually, I think, I'd just leave; he'd know why."

Janet, twenty-eight, body builder

"I'd run for the advice of my best friend. She came to me with that exact problem. My advice was to wait, think it out, and make a plan. Let him have an opportunity to explain. I don't think I would have followed my advice. I'd have left, no argument, no questions, and no more lies or dishonesty. No, it would never work after that."

Deborah, thirty-four, hairdresser

"I'd make a bargain with him: go ahead and fool around, and so will I! If he accepted that plan, I'd walk out."

Rosie, thirty-three, dental technician

"It would depend on what the circumstances were, whether it was a one-night stand or a regular thing. Forgiveness might be possible if he were drunk. He's helpless after too many. Then, I'd make sure he stopped drinking."

Linda, forty-one, data processor

"It's happened to me. Friends told me to ignore it. That was impossible. I began looking more closely at his clothing, taking notes on his late evenings 'at work,' and even dropped in a few times during Saturday golf. Finally, after telling him

I knew, he grudgingly came clean. We decided to see a marriage counselor and things seem to be working out."

Gretta, thirty-nine, bank employee

"I might stay, but it would be the *laissez faire* situation for him . . . no touching me until he did a lot of explaining, begging and promising. He's fun and it's easy to see how others could be attracted to him. But I keep fit and glamorous; he should have no complaints. If he wants to cheat, he'll have to do it without me."

Becky, forty-three, housewife

"I'm a Christian and he's a Christian and, if the devil got into his soul causing him to weaken, I'd understand. The Lord will aid us if we truly love each other and I'd pray he had the strength not to submit. Of course, as a Christian, I can forgive, but even an awful lot of prayer might not make me *forget*."

Beth, thirty-four, caterer

Many had similar viewpoints: they'd either leave or, if not, be unable to completely trust again. If this should happen to you, it seems you alone must decide. Yes, many lonely people are married to or are involved in a long-term commitment with a deceiving mate. You must determine whether to stay in your present situation and continue being unhappy, or to take a chance on *not* being lonely.

Of the 200 women interviewed, 158 opted for staying. Of those, 110 felt "things would never be the same." Twenty-seven felt they could "forgive and forget." Many said they would forgive but hardly ever forget. Sixteen said they would stay but would run constant checks on their husbands and "they had better be where they said they were!" Thirty-two felt they would "try to work things out" but weren't certain they could cope with the hurt and distrust cast upon them by a cheating mate.

One year later I called back upon forty of these women, the ones I felt were the most interesting. Some were in the same situation, still married and trying to cope. Some, the ones who were more difficult to locate, were the ones who had divorced or separated. About half were living in the home once occupied by their mate. The other half, mostly apartment dwellers, had moved and my research took a bit longer. The following quotes were actually from one year to about a year and three months after the initial interview.

FROM THE WIVES WHO LEFT:

"First thing I did was check with my doctor to make certain the rodent hadn't given me herpes or some other communicable venereal disease."

"I went to his boss, his friends and parents. That rotten sonofabitch didn't get off that light. No! He *paid* for ruining my life."

"I wish him well. I really do. He'll have to work hard for years before he can afford to even think about marrying again and screwing around. My attorney took him for everything he had."

"I'm just going to forget as best I can. We had six wonderful years, four that I enjoyed playing the role of wife and mother. When I found out he was cheating, the last two were pure hell. I'm out now and will look forward to what lies ahead."

"I'm having a wonderful time. I never realized how

much fun there is out there in the world and how truly unhappy I was for so long. Everyone should evaluate their situation on a yearly basis and either make it more fun, more loving, more interesting, or just leave."

"For twenty-five years I thought of myself as a 'plain' housewife and mother. I'm still a mother; the kids visit me often. Me? It's a whole new world. Believe it or not I am attractive and even desirable, and I'm almost fifty. Who would have dreamed that fifty could feel so young? There are still so many new things to do and learn."

"He did me a favor, the jerk. Too bad I didn't find out about him and his lying ways sooner. My life is now fun, with all kinds of nice new people. Oddly enough, many men are in the same situation as I. They understand my feelings. It's nice sharing things with my new friends. It's a great life!"

"I still think of him often. We had such a nice life and it was ruined because he couldn't keep his pants zipped. He calls once in a while and we talk. He asks to come over to spend the night, but the hurt doesn't go away that easily. No thank you! Sure there's a weakness, but recalling that past hurt helps forgiving too quickly, thus chancing having to suffer additional anguish. We are going to dinner this coming Friday and he wants me to go on vacation with him for the holidays. Do you think that would be ok? You *do?* You mean if I still love him and he loves me, we might work something out? Goodness, I hope so. Thanks."

Now, let's read what the men had to say.

"I'd break her nose, break the guy's jaw, and leave."
Rick, forty-six, bricklayer

"I'd have to think of the times I've had thoughts of going

They've Been Cheating On You

with someone else and try to analyze our relationship. Had I been rude to her? Selfish of her needs? Yeah, we'd have to talk about it. Maybe there was a good reason she was being unfaithful. Then I would try to forgive her, but I don't know if I could."

Andrew, twenty-eight, accountant

"I don't think I could bear to look at her again without vomiting. I love her too much and I trust her. If she cheated on me my ego and my heart would be broken. I'd just break it off without an explanation and find someone who was faithful."

Robert, thirty-two, salesperson

"I've been unfaithful a few times, and have never been caught. But why would my wife cheat on me? If she did, I'd just smack her around a few times and throw her ass out."

Tom, twenty-five, student/idiot

"I've caught her *five* different times with a man at a motel. It was never the same man. She refused to discuss it with me. I searched my soul for an answer to her unfaithfulness. I talked with her about it and explained her obligations to me and our two children. I did my best to give her reasons not to cheat, then forgot about it and took her word it would never happen again."

Wilbur, thirty-two, asshole

"Who cares? I'm not married to her, not even engaged; only going steady. I've been thinking about doing the same thing; but I would still make her pay. I'd 'get' her best friend (she's made passes at me anyway), and take pictures and show them to my cheating girlfriend —then take my things to the apartment next door and throw the wildest parties the world has ever seen. Naw, she wouldn't cheat on me, but if she did, I'd do what I said, then probably belt her, too."

Bill, thirty-two, department store manager

"Sure I'd be hurt and feel badly for a long time; we've been together over three years and are planning to get married. Guess it would be better to find out now. Still, I'd be crushed. Maybe moving would be a good idea. I wouldn't want to see her or talk to her ever again. It would take a long time before I could try a relationship with someone else. I would also be more cautious and tell my new companion what would be expected from the relationship and what I would do if she ever strayed."

Gregory, thirty-three, writer

"My wife admitted to having an affair — ten years ago. Why in the *hell* couldn't she have just not mentioned it? It hurts as much now as if it just happened. She's sorry for it, but I think, more sorry she told me. She said 'it was bothering her.' Well it sure as hell bothers *me!* We've been married over twenty friggin' years. Why bust up our home? The kids (all three of 'em) are just about on their own and I still love her. Hopefully, my psychiatrist can help me get a good night's sleep again. I hope other wives either don't cheat or, if it was years ago, forget it, huh?"

Griff, forty-two, plumbing contractor

"If my girl cheats on me, then it's only fair because I do it all the time. I'm a tennis pro, you know, and see wives and girlfriends cheating every day. Married to someone, though, I'd expect them to be true and, well, I'd certainly do my best to be faithful, too. But lots of pretty ladies come into my net, and I just might continue to play."

Bert, twenty-six, destined for trouble

Of the 125 men interviewed, most had the same answer. One hundred and six would leave their wives or girlfriends and end the relationship. Of those, seventy-two said they would use some form of physical violence — from slapping their mate to "kicking them in the ass" to breaking their nose. Sixty-four claimed they would "destroy things." Twenty-four stated they'd just leave and not ever see their mates again. The nineteen guys who said they would stay with their cheating mates and try to work things out all admitted "things wouldn't be the same," with one exception: Wilbur, the asshole. He just *knew* his wife would stay home and away from motels.

Six months after my initial interview with the men, my intuition led me back to the ones I felt were noteworthy. I placed several identifying marks as I typed out their recorded interviews.

It was more difficult locating the men. From the twenty who had discovered their wives cheating, or were caught cheating, sixteen were no longer with their spouses. One of the four who were still together was Wilbur. He was still caring for the kids and waiting for his wife with dinner while she continued to keep late hours.

The first separated male I located was Griff, the plumbing contractor. He was living in an apartment just a few blocks from his home. He was attending therapy classes, trying to forget his wife mentioning her affair. He said he needed to be away from her until he could cope. He was a wreck. He cried during much of the interview. I wished him well and left.

Tom, the student, got caught cheating and his girlfriend walked out. He still resided in the same apartment and boasted of a phonebook with at least twenty females listed. Tom was not yet mature enough to make a commitment. At least, not for several more years.

Rick, the bricklayer, was still living in the same untidy apartment his wife of a few months left him in. He vowed "if he caught her cheating, he'd break her nose, break the guy's jaw, and leave." As it happened, he watched from the window as his wife got out of a car after giving the driver a friendly kiss on the cheek. Rick stormed out, dragged the guy from the car, and proceeded to beat him to a pulp. The police intervened before he caught up with his wife. Unfortunately, his wife's *brother* was the driver of the car. Rick's insane jealousy was bound to have eventually destroyed his marriage, anyway, agree?

Bill, the department store manager who "felt no particular obligation," was now living with his girlfriend, although he still felt no urge to keep a commitment. In fact, he admitted flirting with others so often that his girlfriend finally asked him to leave. Bill did so only to find himself crying the blues over his old, true love. She began dating *his* best friend and "from all that appears to be," he told, "they're getting along pretty good." I asked what plans he had for the future. "I dunno," he replied. "Guess I'll just see what comes up next."

Bert, the tennis pro, also had a new companion. Bert was found out by the husband of one of his pupils and lost his girl *and* job. However, undaunted, he set up shop at a new club several miles from his former employer. Bert, like Tom, needed more time and experience to "age" him a bit. He too seemed like the kind to stay single until he was too old to look good on the courts.

SPOTTING THE CHEATER

The chore of spotting someone practiced in the art of deceiving isn't an easy one. Oftentimes, cheating is second nature to some people. Many of us realize our mate might be cheating, but tend to let things go until there is evidence or we "catch them in the act." Here are some easy clues to look for:

1. Has their schedule, all of a sudden, *changed?* Are they getting home *later* than before or leaving *earlier?* Spending more time at the office, but you never can seem to reach them there?

2. Do they begin bragging about a certain secretary or salesman at the office? This could be a sign of attraction to this person, or, they would like you to be more *like* this person. Maybe you don't have the same degree of ambition as before. Perhaps your tidiness is not what it once was, in combing your hair or shaving or wearing neat clothes. This could be a hint to shape up.

3. They are always looking at the opposite sex. Of course, if the rule is "no touching," it might take an awful lot of "looking" to counter that handicap. Looking is OK; ogling is *not*. This tends to make you jealous and perhaps, as we said, they are "trying to tell you something," or maybe they are about to wander.

4. Does your mate tend to hang on others at parties, leaving you standing in the center of the room — lost? Are there times he or she disappears for more than a few minutes, then suddenly comes over to spend a few minutes before taking off on another chase? Maybe they are extremely extroverted! Is there the need for an ego boost from others that they just don't get at home? Could this effort be to arouse jealousy and attract notice? Maybe they want others to think they are still desirable by someone other than their spouse. And maybe they are "nailing" or are "getting nailed" by every person who walks, crawls, or flies.

5. The breath might also be a clue. Is there an odor like smoke or liquor on unspecified occasions? Or, is their breath too sweet-smelling, like mint or Binaca, upon arrival at home?

6. Obvious hints are a smudge of lipstick on his collar or stockings in her purse and not on her legs. Even *more* obvious is a lack of interest in making love as often as in the past. Look at yourself to see if it's you who is less desirable, less interested, or more demanding. If it isn't you, it's *them!* Something is happening, and you should look a bit more deeply for a reason.

7. Watch for little pieces of paper with phone numbers scratched on them without names, or maybe ticket stubs of some kind, or credit card receipts to hotels or restaurants on the far end of town. I'm not advocating a "body search." Just be aware of these inconspicuous clues.

8. If your telephone rings and the caller hangs up, it's annoying, but hardly reason to "call out the posse." A sudden influx of "wrong number" calls might be cause to wonder. Or, if your mate abruptly ends a conversation and suddenly hangs up when you walk into the room, *something* is up.

9. A more subtle clue is, after hounding you to lose weight for an extended period of time, quite unexplainably, they stop mentioning it altogether. Either your mate has decided they just don't care anymore — or there's someone else on the side who doesn't *have* a weight problem.

10. Experienced cheaters know *when* to pick a fight and leave. Often an argument is planned to coincide with prior plans to meet someone. This leaves the spouse home alone and upset, while the philanderer is out having fun with the person they *really* wanted to be with. This, through interviews with male scoundrels, was found to be a common ploy.

11. An even more difficult change to recognize is when spouses *increase* their attention and lovemaking to their mates. Having "someone on the side" doesn't necessarily decrease

their hormonal urges. They could be trying to mask their infidelity. After all, you're not as exciting as their new playtoy. Yes, they could show more attention at home and certainly in the presence of friends or relatives.

BEWARE OF ALL CHANGES

Whew! There are so many things to look for! But nobody said it was easy to find and maintain a happy relationship. Sooner or later all cheaters will betray themselves. Some will become too complacent and careless. Others want to get caught for a variety of reasons. It is hoped that the clues spelled out on the previous pages will enlighten you and will shorten the time this unfaithful person has of robbing you of a loving and trusting life with someone else.

I implore you, if you have had the sad experience of someone you cared for cheating on you, read more of this book. It is so helpful in solving many things that can cause you *to* be lonely and show you so many ways *not* to be lonely.

Remember: being disappointed — hurting — is natural. There are few things *anyone* can tell you or that you can read that will stop the hurting. Most simply have to go through this mourning period. If it lasts weeks, to as long as a few months, that again is normal. It's called *situational* loneliness. Just don't let this hurt last too long. If it does, it can turn into *chronic* loneliness. When you recognize this is happening to you, please, *please* seek professional help. It will be the best money you've ever spent.

Chapter Four

Temporary Breakup

You and your companion of almost two years have decided to "cool it" for a while to "gather your thoughts" and to "get your heads on straight." I've heard these sayings before and was never able to qualify them. Does it mean your thoughts are scattered? That maybe you are in need of psychiatric help? Is your head *bent* or crooked? Does it mean you are tired of your present romantic involvement and want to get away for some "alone" time to think things out? Or does it signify you are entering a relationship with someone new and this is a hint to your mate that the end is near?

Whatever the reason, let's just say you two still have strong feelings for each other but have not been able to discuss your problems intelligently or satisfactorily. The end result is that you are going to be alone. The first or second night is bearable, but now, after that third night, you are both alone and lonely. You miss the routine, the habit of being with someone. Your partner of over 700 days has not come through that door in seventy-two hours. Yes, there is a change, even a temporary one — so how to handle it?

The nights haven't all been sleepless — but almost. What is he/she doing? Talk a bit to the mirror, ask questions, and try to search out an answer. Is it love? If so, why are we apart? Is there someone else? Should I be with someone else? How much longer before we get back together? Or will we? The mirror, as usual, doesn't have an answer. People at the office notice a bit of sluggishness; you're not as happy as usual. Friends ask if you're feeling well or "What's wrong?" The decision is to tell them you're each "taking time out to think things through." The relationship has come to a standstill.

Upon making the grave error of asking co-workers for advice, chances are the response is not what you want to hear. The office "sweetpea" will exclaim to you what a *wonderful* couple you both seemed to be or how much in love you both looked at a recent office party, but will offer no suggestions on what to do about it. The office bitch will say, "Good riddance to bad rubbish! I always *did* think he was a loser and you were too good for him!" She'll just be happy *you* are unhappy. Then, there's the office turd who couldn't make out in a women's prison with a handful of pardons. He will offer no advice but will hurriedly ask you out, hoping to catch you on the rebound. Your best friend will say to "take it slow and not make any profound moves," and to "go home and give it some thought." *This* advice is sound. Three days is not a sufficient mourning period for a profound move. In fact, there's no set rule on this, except that within five days or a week I would begin to panic. If the separation has lasted a few weeks or longer, things may never work out.

You're back in the apartment having a snack, listening to some music and thinking. Apparently, one of you is not able to communicate feelings. What is the reason for the split up? Why not place a call and talk about it? If you care, you'll want to shorten this "hurt period" and begin living happily. Or, if it isn't going to work out, try to find out as quickly as you can and not simmer in limbo. Why couldn't this have been discussed *before* the split? You could have possibly solved the dilemma together *before* one offered the other the door. I hope it sounds reasonable to you, because it does to me!

If no call is made, but there's a feeling deep down that your companion will be back, this is the time to be very careful of any actions. One error might deter any chance of reconciliation. In fact, the things *not* to do seem to overshadow the things *to* do. My suggestion is to be active or go nuts, but choose activity helpful to you, while not being harmful to your maybe-renewed relationship. Perhaps go to dinner or a movie with a friend, sister or brother — *no* other escort that might remotely be a "contender" for your affections. No blind dates and no one-night stands; you know what I mean. *Keep busy!* Go to a class or seminar. Use the spare time productively. Put in overtime at work. But be good, because when he comes back, he'll want to know he can still trust you. The same goes for the guys. *You*, my unthinking or uncompromising friend, must make certain *you* don't commit a similar error. Having a date, even what we term a harmless one, could cause hurt feelings and long-term resentments. What's good for the goose should also be good for the gander, right? No more "the guy can get away with it" crap. No, sir! We are in an era of *equality!*

AN ACADEMIC LIST

While alone, take the time to think out what the future holds for the relationship. Try dealing with it *academically*. Make a list of your likes and dislikes. Go over what you want and *need* in a person. If this relationship isn't right, it just might take some heartache and being honest with yourself. You have to deal from the *head* as well as from the *heart* and look at what is best for you! If you *fake* being happy, it will result in unhappiness for both of you.

When making this list, put down that "he watched TV all the time and ate too much and snored when he slept." Or you, fella, put down that she had that noisy music playing all the time and you really can't stand her two best friends. You might be the right *wrong* people for each other. Things might be comfortable, but not exciting — and everyone needs excitement. Laziness often prevents you from making a change; enduring is simpler.

"Scoundrels, like great earthquakes, have a fatal fascination," someone once said. That wrong person could be fun and exciting and really teach you things: love, loving, heartache, *pain*, how to cope, tolerate, laugh and maybe even how to choose the *right* person. Look in those dark corners of the closet for letters from the past. They'll give you an insight on what to be doing now. Yes, history does have a way of repeating itself. These hidden mementos will bring back nice memories of being wooed and won, or maybe your own handwritten notes you wrote but neglected to mail will open your eyes. "I'll marry you anywhere, anytime. I'd rather die than live without you." How many times have we heard that? Even in my moderate wanderings, I could be tried for second-degree murder *several dozen times* with words like "I can't live without you" from ardent admirers, all, I might add, who are still alive and either with someone else, or still trying to find Mr. Right.

But you, each of you, must understand that life is an experience — a host of experiences — and hopefully you'll learn from each one. If your relationship is comfortable but dull, please talk it out and see where the problem areas lie. If, for some reason or other, they can't be *talked* out, then how can you ever expect to *work* them out?

Women might ask: Is he comfortable to be with? Dependable? Is excess smoking or drinking a problem? Can he be trusted? What about getting along well with my friends and parents? Does he have a future with his company? Do we have fun together? What about a family? Will he ever stop watching TV and pay attention to me? Will he include me in his weekends and not always be playing golf or tennis or off fishing or hunting "with the boys"? Do I love him? Do I *like* him? He has some bad habits, but I can live with those, can't I? It's wise to make a list of those questions. A short pencil is more accurate than a long memory.

Do you see the dozens and *dozens* of questions that will help you to decide? Yeah, some guys are right and some are wrong, and some are *more* wrong. For some reason these "more wrong" guys seem to be the ones who know what to say, how to treat you, how to make you "feel." They are the kind who make you laugh and happy and tingly, but something inside them is missing. They don't want a commitment, but would rather go through life laughing and being charming, debonaire, sweet, thoughtful, macho, and *single*. They'll allow you to like 'em, love 'em, experience 'em, learn from 'em — but *not* to establish a life with them. They are transitory and should be recognized and treated as such.

And *you*, Mr. Unable-to-talk-it-out-with-your-girlfriend, what kind of list do *you* plan to make? Here are some pointers. Is she sweet to you most of the time? Do you like her? Does she accept your friends? Even the one who always makes a few casual remarks about "what he would do if she were his," or the one who smokes all the time, making the apartment smell like a boiler room on a tramp steamer? And that other one who just "drops" by now and then when you'd rather be alone? Do you like many of the same things? Music, food, movies, vacation spots, sports or hobbies? What about *kids?* Does she want three and you none? And do you laugh together? Love satisfactorily? Are you able to agree on plans for the future? The list is endless. Pick out the important things, the major problems. Perhaps you're both in a rut and have

Temporary Breakup

been staying home every night doing nothing. *Make* that list and *act!* There are so many wonderful things going on in the world that you two should be a part of, things you can enjoy and *share.*

Get on that telephone and just talk for a while. See how she feels. Invite her for lunch tomorrow. She'll accept. At lunch, be on time. Be nice. Help her with the chair, maybe bring a flower. Touch her arm, her hand, her hair. Demonstrate the most sorrowful look you can and stare deeply into those eyes. Let the pain and loneliness residing there show. During this "trial time" life is at a standstill. She is very much in your thoughts and there isn't any room for anyone else to squeeze in. You've been alone four days now — and *nights!* You want her back, and she is feeling the same emotions. After lunch, call her at work and ask her to a movie. When you show up at the door, have a dozen roses or even one rose, and when you come in and embrace, you can forget the movie. Throw the rose on the chair when she throws you on the couch, and you guys are "in for the night."

It *is* smart to be sweet and talk things out. The attentiveness you displayed at lunch has already set the stage for a beautiful new beginning. However, don't think for one moment, Mr. Right, that one tumble on the couch will settle things. No deal! She will want to *talk,* buddy, to make certain the problem areas will either become nonexistent or will be worked on. This is the time to be "cool." Don't make love and figure everything is OK. Everything might *seem* to be OK, but it is only a delightful pause between rounds. No, pal, there won't be much sleep tonight, but not from amorous adventures. Instead there'll be questions and answers and *plans.* She might even whip out the list. And that's how it should be. If you think differently, you're only kidding yourself. Don't be too hasty, trying to "win the battle" and end up "losing the war." She wants to know why you don't take her out to lunch *other* than special occasions or only after a breakup. Be prepared with convincing answers. Isn't romance wonderful? Isn't being together with someone you love and like so very satisfying?

SIGN A TREATY TOGETHER

Compromise is the main word in this temporary breakup. Sit down like heads-of-state when a peace treaty is signed. Just remember, be sincere and work out plans that can be followed. There is no sense in promising her you'll never take a night out with the boys again or that *certainly* you'll invite her mother to the theater with you when Dad is out of town. And, no, you can't really smell the cat-shit odor in her kitchen and even if you could it wouldn't bother you. Or you, Little Miss Perfect, find out what bothers *him* and see if it can be worked out. Yes, compromise. Try not to promise the impossible, but just "trim the edges" off some of the big complaints. Chances are things will work out for everyone. On the other hand, if making up isn't that easy, here is a list of other things to do and not to do:

1. Send a cutesy little card, maybe with an "I miss you" written on it. No need for a signature.

2. Do *not* call the office and become a nuisance. *No* late-night phone calls. If neither can sleep, let it go at that. If you *really* can't take this late night pain, maybe one sweet call, and hope it works. But no repeated calls, OK?

3. When talking, don't threaten to go with other people. Maybe, just maybe, you can say that you "plan to be away for a week on vacation." *That* should warrant a response.

4. Do *not* make demands over the telephone and don't make any accusations. It just might be a time for artful negotiations. State your position as unemotionally as possible. Be calm. Re-

member this is a stressful time for both of you. Be understanding.

5. Bring up reminders of those special nights when this or that was so wonderful, or other fun times you've shared.

6. Someone must take the initiative. Just grasp their hand, look into their eyes and say: "I miss you and I love you and I hurt so badly without you I just feel like dying." *That* will get their attention. It *works!* Just make certain you are sincere. There is no need to fake a tear. If you truly miss them, tears are automatic. Guys are suckers for tears. And girls, if your man shows a sign of wetness in the eyes, you can't resist, can you?

LOVE IS THE ANSWER

But let's not misinterpret pity or habit, or the fear of being alone, as love or a reason for renewing a relationship. Pity is short-termed. If it's only "feeling sorry" for this nice guy or gal, it isn't sufficient reason to sustain a relationship. No, you need a "working" relationship. If two people who care for each other and want to work things out to a mutual satisfaction can discuss their problems openly, *truthfully,* they certainly have a chance. Good luck to you. With care, trust, negotiating, and compromise, you'll make it. Now, a little story:

Not too long ago, while I visited with a friend on the front porch of his country home, two of his friends pulled up in a pickup truck. We were talking about my manuscript as the two visitors came onto the porch. Upon mentioning the subject of the book, Tim, the bearded visitor, came over and, like so many others I had talked to, said, "I need to read that." Tim had a desperate look in his eyes. It was easy to detect his torment. Pulling me off to the side as though I was his savior, he sought answers to his problems.

Tim was about 5′9″ tall, medium build, thirty years old, and looked a little unpolished. He was a contractor, building small homes on the water in this particular rural era. He was open in relating his story because he was in pain and needed someone to help. His best friend had just committed suicide the week before. "He was buried just yesterday afternoon," Tim said with reddened eyes. "He just gave up. His wife left him and he was out of a job and he just didn't want no more of it."

Tim looked into my eyes, took a deep breath, and admitted he too had come close to suicide at least a dozen times. He confessed to having sold every gun he owned because "many times I just sat with the gun to my head or with the barrel of the rifle in my mouth and knew that someday I'd just pull the trigger." This concerned me to the point I hesitated in giving any type of advice. Tim needed professional help. When I didn't say anything, Tim became disturbed. "Please don't be like those psychiatrists I've gone to. They just sit and ask questions and nod their heads. I've spent lots of money with them and still don't have any answers." Obviously, more time was needed to get to the root of Tim's problems. But apparently, Tim was impatient.

What could I do for him? This grown man was in front of me trying to seek something to ease his pain, and all I could say was see a professional person and try to cope with it. His eyes were begging for an answer. I thought I might act as a friend and do what I could.

"What is your situation right now with your loved one?" I asked.

"My wife of six years just left me last week. She has a seven-year-old son who calls me 'Daddy' and has only known me as his father. She talks to me, but she doesn't want to have anything to do with me. I just screwed up."

"How?" I inquired.

"Well, I hit her a few times. I have a bad temper, but she

Temporary Breakup 47

has come back to me anyway a dozen or so times — but I keep screwing up."

I decided to throw out a few stories of my own, hoping he might identify with them. "Hell, Tim, I know how it is. I've been single about twenty-five years of my life and have done things I'm *very* ashamed of. The thing is," I continued, seeing I had his attention and was gaining a type of kinship with him and his problem, "I was too young and too stupid to recognize that I was cruel, unfair, and selfish. I ran off at least a dozen truly good girls by being a jackass; by getting a little too drunk or too jealous or by trying to change them. And there were times that I couldn't control my temper."

Tim was listening intently. "I did that too," he said. "When the mood struck I would throw things or break the TV or pull the door off the hinges and she don't want no more of it."

"Hey man," I put my hand on his shoulder, "*lots* of guys do that, the ones who are hot-heads. They're sorry for it the next day and they wish they had another chance. But then, within a few weeks, they do it again."

"Right, *right!*" he answered, as though I had found the key to unlock a secret door. "I've gone back and promised not to do something and kept doing it. She don't want to have nothing to do with me no more," he repeated. "But she called today and wants to see me tonight."

"Then," I answered, "you *do* still have a chance. Some women will take it once, maybe twice. Some will take it — the weak ones — forever. You're lucky, my friend. You're aware of your problem and you want help, but I'm afraid it's going to depend on *you*, Tim."

Tim began spewing forth information like you would never believe. He said he had done everything in the past few years after a breakup. He said he cried, he begged, he promised, and within a few weeks of his being back, he did the same thing again. I told him to spill his heart out to her as he was doing with me.

"Play it one day at a time, Tim," I advised. "Take her to a quiet restaurant tonight, hold her hand, tell her you love her and you want her and you're sorry — no tears. She's seen, you tell me, all the tears she can handle from you. So just be truthful about it and tell her, with all the sincerity you can muster into one bearded face, that you *will* try.

"And, Tim, *do* try. You have most of the fight won because you *know* you're the one who's at fault and you *know* you've made her unhappy. And what about this little boy you love so dearly? Surely you've made life miserable for him too. If you love either of them, either straighten up or get the hell out of their lives forever."

This was working on Tim. He admitted to having two other wives, each for but a short time, because he had done the same things to alienate them. I had heard all I needed to hear from Tim. Whatever I would tell him now would be redundant, and time was limited. He was to see his estranged wife in less than one hour. I suggested he forgive himself and try to feel better about himself and truly believe he could — and had — changed. I wasn't trying to play "doctor." I knew there was little time, and I prayed for a miracle.

That evening, Tim did meet with his wife and they talked. He apparently told her some of what I had suggested and the dinner was a momentary success — all depending on whether Tim could control his temper. I had advised him to "take it easy, make his wife feel safe and at ease with him, and not to try to push for an immediate response." Tim did just that. They saw each other several more times that week and continued to "date" for a short period of time.

A month passed. Tim called and we visited. He doesn't have his macho beard any longer, and he doesn't look as tough anymore. I told him I thought women wanted a man to be strong — when it was necessary. I told him they certainly wanted to feel safe, as though their loved one could protect them, but what they wanted most was kindness and gentleness and a man who was sensitive.

Temporary Breakup

Three months passed. Tim again came to visit me and said they were working things out. He was taking it one day at a time and, for the first time he could ever remember, he felt happy and thought his wife and son were also happy. He thanked me for "putting him straight."

The real person, I reasoned, that Tim was about to find happiness with was, mostly, Tim. And his analyst certainly was a big factor, even if Tim didn't want to credit him for it. Perhaps Tim stopped attending just a few visits short of finding the answer. Then I, luckily, happened into his life and, by more luck, gave Tim some suggestions that proved beneficial to him.

And that truly *is* the reason for this book. I'm just a human who has lived "out there" in the same world as you. I suffered and made mistakes and experienced much of what many of you are now going through. And I went for professional help on more than one occasion. What I learned from these professionals, from hundreds of interviews and from my own experience, I'm relating in this text.

When things go wrong it feels as though the world will end. It won't! Keep a positive attitude, a fun sense of humor, and know that you'll be alive tomorrow. Nobody dies from a broken heart; it just seems like it. Take life one step at a time. After you talk things out and think them out, chances are you'll be together again.

Chapter Five

Divorce

Divorce is often more hurtful than being widowed. People think they have failed. But this is not necessarily true. Many "good" people divorce. Maybe they're just not *good* for each other.

There are many reasons for wives wanting to divorce what we might label a "fine" husband, other than money and sex (or the lack of it). Often the man who becomes involved in his business simply forgets his *home life* is a large part of his life also. He, as many of us do, takes things for granted.

EXAMPLE "A": EDITH AND ARCHIE

Archie: "I loved her and asked her to marry me. I work hard, never stray, and have been a good provider. We have two cars, a country home. The kids go to fine schools. We go on a couple of vacations a year and have a wonderful marriage."

Maybe, Mr. Perfect Husband, you come home, pat the wife on the head, kiss the dog, and settle into your "Archie" chair. Maybe, other than those two vacations per year you mention so proudly, you neglect the other forty-eight or so weeks doing *your* thing. So you go to dinner a few times a month at a fine restaurant. Big deal! Do you two *communicate?* Do you *share* moments with each other? Or do you run off to play golf or fish every weekend the weather is suitable and leave her home alone with the kids and the housework? You know, fella, she might just be your maid, house cleaner, dishwasher, laundress, and warm blanket for cold nights — and she might not like this role.

After being married for fourteen years, much of the romance has simply vanished. You aren't as neat as back when you shaved before going to bed rather than only in the morning to prepare for work. When was the last time you took some time to listen to how *her* day went, and tried to put a little romance back in your life? How often do you bring little gifts other than for her birthday, Christmas, etc.? How about taking a few weekends every year when the weather is perfect for fishing or golfing, and do things *she* might want to share with you? Perhaps just because she doesn't complain or bitch at you all of the time, you think things are OK, and just go on living your dull "existence" day after day. Guess you never thought of those things before, have you? No, guess not. Well, your eyes are certainly open wide now, aren't they? Now you'll take a look at the lady you've taken for granted for these many years.

You just came home and when you reached out to give your spouse a loving "pat," she backed away. When you ignored that and flopped into the "Bunker" seat, a beer wasn't brought out immediately. Nevertheless, you shrugged (you're not the excitable kind) and went on reading the evening paper and watching TV at the same time, waiting for that melodious voice to call you for dinner. She is in the backyard breaking up a fight between the two boys and trying to get them to clean up before eating. Then, your daughter has seemingly *welded* her head to the telephone and presents yet another problem to settle. You suddenly lift your head and look around to discover it's at least fifteen minutes past the usual call to sit down and stuff your face. After shrugging again and patiently waiting another five minutes or so, you push the paper aside, turn the TV remote to "mute" and call, "Edith!" This is routine, isn't it, Archie? But not today. Today a *surprise* is waiting. All is quiet, the kids are upstairs in their rooms, and Edith comes down and stands in front of you, feet planted, jaw set, and arms folded.

"Archie, I've given this a lot of thought and I want a divorce!"

What is this person saying? In a fraction of a second your brain goes over how good you are and what could possibly have gone wrong. Surely she's kidding! Just look at her. She's never acted this way before — *ever!* "Are these words coming from the lips of my little princess?" you ask. Sit up straight in the chair, take a deep gulp, put the paper down, and listen. Too late now, buddy. Complacency has lasted a little too long, and there is *nothing* you can say or do to change her mind. Tonight, you either sleep in one of the boys' rooms or go to a motel. Tomorrow, little Edith is filing for divorce.

What to do? This life of comfort and security is over. There was no time to hide the extra cash; everything in your marriage was above board. You have been found guilty of being dull and boring and selfish; your butt is being shanghaied into *bachelorhood* without warning.

Now the fun begins. *Anything* for another chance. You'll go *with* Edith to visit her parents. You'll offer to take her fishing or golfing *with* you the next time. Go one step further: *give up* golf or fishing. Watch TV only a few hours a night and not *all* night *every* night. Shave *before* you get into bed with her, and bathe too. Next year let *her* choose the vacation spot. That's it! *She* can choose where to go and it doesn't have to be that leaky mountain cabin you call a country home, stuck in the middle

Divorce 53

of nowhere. Yes, go to Acapulco or Hawaii or even Paris! Promise *anything* . . . while in the back of your mind you just *know* — the very second you get her back, after a few weeks — it will be the same routine for the family, back to doing what you want while she assumes the role of referee with the kids, cleaning, dull evenings doing needlepoint, and preparing those special meals of blubber-producing calories you like so much. Things are now back to normal. Well, she isn't going for it. She might have been dumb to say "I do" to you fourteen years ago, but that doesn't mean she is *still* dumb. No, buddy, you are soon to be a divorced man.

Edith: Edith has made a wise decision — or *has* she? You still love him, don't you, Edith? Of course you do, but just happen not to *like* him very much, right? You know, Edith, good men are hard to come by. Perhaps you were a little harsh with him. You *could* have mentioned this to him when the first signs showed trouble ahead. You could have tried to work it out. A marriage counselor (after you've talked it over with your best friend — we all do) might have helped. Maybe even a threat or two would have opened ole Archie's eyes years ago. Perhaps you are being too hasty. He does love you and *is* loyal to you. He has no really bad habits, or at least, none that couldn't be discussed and perhaps rectified.

Think about it a bit more, Edith. About not only the kids, but about *your* life after Archie has left the scene. Are you going to have to go to work? Is there enough money to live comfortably until you meet someone else? Maybe this someone else will have larger inadequacies or more deficiencies. Yeah, Edith, call ole Archie back and try to work things out. Better yet, before you get in that goal-line stance, corner him and put down a few ultimatums, a few new rules. *Voice* your opinion. The guy's OK, just dull and preoccupied with work and selfish with free time. *Whatever* you can't live with, *discuss* it first. Teach him!

EXAMPLE "B": BOB AND CATHY

Let's take another example of a husband and wife problem. Bob is the perfect husband who does all the right things, but one day a friend tells you Bob has been seen making semimonthly trips to another friend's house for a "nooner." Everybody knows about it, but as a friend, she thought she would tell you. "He's making such a fool of you, Cathy, and you should know about it." Let's not be angry with the friend. Perhaps she does mean well and has thought about telling you for a long time. Yes, as hurting as the news is, she might be a very *good* friend.

What to do? Divorce him? Shoot the cheating, lying slob? Forget about it and pretend it didn't happen? Confront him? Go see his semimonthly "punch" and threaten to tell her husband? Whew! That's an individual thing, but let's suppose you *did* confront him and begged him not to lie anymore or deny it. He'll stammer and stutter and make up all sorts of reasons he was there (probably thought out ahead of time in the event he was seen) and try to worm his way out. He loves you and wants to stay married to you. Thing is, he'd like to catch a little piece on the side — and what you don't know, won't hurt you.

But the sad fact is you *do* know. You *don't* believe him. He lied when you asked him not to, and now you're aware of it. Memory recalls the many times he was late, "busy at the office and slept in his chair," when you felt sorry for the hardworking sweetheart and offered him extra comfort when he came home. Where was he? How about the times you went into the bedroom and the conversation he was having on the phone ended abruptly? It sounded a bit "strange," but not anymore. It was *her* he was talking to. That dirty SOB won't change. He doesn't deserve another chance. He'll abstain for a week or two, maybe a month, but you'll have to hide a transmitter in his *navel* to keep track of him. You can never trust him again.

There's no reason to live the remainder of your life this way. You're only thirty-three and attractive. Lots of men would welcome a new wife with the qualifications you have. Not even a talk with a marriage counselor would help. It is over: Bob, you are in the past.

Being sensible, you agree to a "trial separation." He spends a full month in the hotel and comes over for dinner and to visit with the kids a few times a week. Still being pissed at him, forgiveness is not present in your thoughts. It is *over!* When he calls on the phone, the mere sound of his whining voice disgusts you. When he tries to be nice, you attack with the ferocity of a starving buzzard. It's impossible to imagine how you loved him in the first place. Now's the time for a new life.

Your "mourning period" is not a problem; revenge is. You have three general choices:

1. You "cool it" for a while, file for divorce, hire a smart attorney to strip Bob of whatever you can, and resume life being a mother. In time, someone will "find you," a person who can appreciate you, and you'll end up remarried and happy.

2. You go on the prowl. Plan smartly and still take the kids to Little League, but now you become aware of the father of one of the boys, the one who always seems to be alone. You never noticed him before. He just clapped when your son had a pop fly bounce off his head and joined in with the other "moms" yelling at the unfair umpire, even if "little Johnny" was out by a mile. Soon it's time to look up a local "Parents Without Partners" group. Surely you have a close friend who is also divorced and the two of you can go to some parties or clubs together. Maybe you can get lucky and find some divorced guy in the neighborhood whose wife moved to Jamaica with the tennis instructor who taught at the club. That would be lucky; the guy is already trained at being a father and husband and needs solace. You two can share sad experiences and end up laughing about it. Yeah, you'll do OK!

3. Go out and "lay" everyone who hesitates, in order to "get even" with Bob. The only thing is, this might hurt *you* more. Psychologists call it "sports fucking." You're not really enjoying it, just doing it to keep busy and help repair your wounded ego. You might want to prove to yourself that you are pretty and desirable. This avenue isn't necessary, but if you take it, I won't judge you. Others might, though, the ones who count. Certainly the kids will catch on to a series of "uncles" staying over for the night. Or they might begin to think they've been adopted by the babysitter if you leave them home too often.

EXAMPLE "C": FINANCIAL PROBLEMS

There are still other problems with divorce. What if there is not enough money to live as you have in the past? What to do with the kids if you can't afford child care? Must life actually stop while you assume the role of nonmarried mother? Must you wait until the kids are grown and on their own before you can look for someone new to share your life? Oh, God! That's at least *ten years* from now!

Solution #1: If you are in this category, face the facts! Circumstances might favor *selling* your present home and moving into a less affluent neighborhood. Part-time work might be necessary. But, then, you have no training in anything other than being a wife and mother, who married Bob fresh out of high school. Then, my dear sweet divorcée, you have to *plan!* There's a lot of legwork to do. First, find a part-time position, hopefully close to home. Next, locate a nearby friend or neighbor who doesn't mind having your well-mannered offspring spend a few hours each evening with their kids. Then, decide on a career and attend school. Maybe the part-time job is one where you can learn while you earn. Well, that wasn't too tough, was it? The hard part is deciding what must be done; the hardest is *doing* it.

Solution #2: Rush out and marry the first guy who asks. Wrong! Being under pressure will prompt many to make unwise, hurried decisions. You might get lucky and find a "good" guy, but the chances against it are too high. No, be careful with your next selection. And when you choose, do so for a number of smart reasons. Find someone who appears to be a good father, someone you like and then love, *not* who is looking for a new place to reside. And *not* an "anxious rebounder." A recently divorced man will only give you more problems. You married the first time for love. This time you are not a schoolgirl anymore, impressed by the captain of the football team. You're a grown woman with responsibilities to your children and to yourself, so decide a bit more practically.

Solution #3: Go live with your parents — or his. Again, this depends on the type of person you are and your relationship with either family. This way, Grandma will welcome being the babysitter while you work and pursue an education and/or a career. Just set the ground rules beforehand; let them know you need and want their help, but that these are *your* kids and you expect them (the grandparents) to follow your instructions as far as rules go. Grandparents *do* spoil their grandchildren.

So you see, there *are* several options. Once you get over being angry and resentful — and time has a way of handling that, in most cases — the healing process is almost complete. The sudden shock of having to do everything by yourself has settled in your mind. Now a decision can be made. Your judgment becomes more reliable, your thinking more clear. High emotions have lessened, and decisions can become academic.

EXAMPLE "D": MARK AND HEATHER

Mark has, after finding Heather had a lover, recently obtained a divorce and full custody of the children. He has been a good father for almost twelve years and now must become a mother also. The two boys aren't much of a problem, Mark can somewhat relate to them, but the girl has to be handled in a special way. Who will comb her hair? Select her clothes? Gulp! Tell her about "becoming a woman"? She's eleven now and beginning to ask questions. What does Mark do about a babysitter when he's at work? The twin boys are only seven and their big sister is just not old enough to handle them; she can barely handle herself.

Well, Mark has to make plans in the same way as the wronged mothers in the preceding pages. They had no experience at being a father either, and it's much the same problem. In the midst of these problems, Mark has to heal, recovering the self-esteem he felt prior to Heather leaving him. There's not a lot of time to feel lonely, with the kids and all, but when these alone moments do come, he hurts. Oh, how he hurts.

Hurt, I'm happy to tell you, seems to be a normal process. It isn't so bad to feel, to want, to open up and cry. Crying can be a cleansing factor. We've all heard in movies, "Go ahead . . . Get it all out." There's truth in that advice for both men and women. The loneliness Mark feels is termed *situational loneliness*. It will last from perhaps weeks to months, but it *will* end. Experts are more concerned with the term *chronic loneliness*, lasting for a year or longer, the kind that leads into almost paralyzing depression and fear of ever recovering. This is the type of loneliness so intense that, if it should happen to you after you've experimented with suggestions from this book, you should seek professional help. There are people who have spent their *lives* in the study of this destructive loneliness and can offer you the most help.

But Mark has too many problems to feel chronic loneliness; there is no time. He will experience deep depression with the loss of his wife and the seeming hoplessness of his situation, but that will soon pass. He will have his work, maybe have his or her parents help with the kids, and his friends will do what they can for him. He can find someone new, if he gets exposure and lets others know he is "on the open market" again. Yes, it all depends on the person who is wounded. They can hurt and feel sorry for themselves and hide out from the world. Or they can do the normal thing and accept this mourning period, but do their utmost to shorten it and begin their new life.

Accepting the fact you are going to get a divorce is often more painful than accepting the *death* of your partner. In death, there are no choices to make; in divorce, there are several.

Are you going to make up again? What about visitation rights with the kids? What happens if he just "drops over" and you have a date? What if you see *him* with a date? Suppose he doesn't pay the child support. Do you send him to jail? Suppose she begins to have a bevy of beaus and you feel it's not good for the kids. Do you go back to court?

You begin to wonder if maybe things couldn't have been worked out. Do you still love her in spite of what she did to you? And maybe you should have given him a chance to explain. Were you too hasty in believing your friend? Perhaps there *was* an explanation . . .

This is the reason I cannot emphasize strongly enough that you must deal with problems from an *academic* standpoint. I'm not advocating that you continue on with a selfish or philandering partner; only that you take time in making a decision. Try to work through your minister, a marriage counselor, or a psychiatrist. It is worth the extra effort on your part. After all, it took a long time and lots of effort and expense to get married, and that may just be a fraction of the cost of getting *un*married.

But, once you are certain divorce is the *only* answer, be prepared for the biggest change in your life. If you've been married several years, perhaps as many as fifteen or twenty, be prepared for a different world out there. I dislike comparing marriage to prison, but the changes the world has gone through since your incarceration into matrimony can be frightening. On the other hand, there have been some good changes too. The main thing is, if you are divorced, learn how *not* to be lonely. Look at your marriage as *one chapter* in your book of life. Continue on with a positive attitude to your next chapter. It may be a more rewarding one.

Chapter Six

How to Forget

This very second there are millions of people involved in unhappy relationships, and they simply don't know what to do. Some of these troubled souls are married. Others just have alliances that have turned sour and they don't know why. If you are involved in a situation that fits this scenario and you want out, know, for certain, that things will not improve. They will only worsen or (God, forbid!) remain the same.

Immediate action must be taken. Yeah, it must be ended. Once it becomes crystal clear you are with someone and unhappy, still lonely, and life is dissatisfying and your heart feels only the thump-thump of blood passing through, it is time to leave and begin to forget. How to go about it? How to make the break?

I know, more time is needed to rehearse a parting speech. You are apprehensive about doing it. You feel guilty and a bit sorry for your partner, right? I say *don't* feel guilty! Fight off that apprehension. Remind yourself again and again that this relationship is not fulfilling. Refuse to waste any more months or years of your life "enduring." The pain and agony are at a breaking point, and the loneliness far overshadows what good might still exist. Keep these thoughts foremost in your mind. They will give you the needed strength to begin a parting speech leading to a new world for you both. Chances are your partner is experiencing the same dilemma and hasn't the courage to act. It is neither bright nor fair to remain in limbo as each lonely, non-fulfilling day passes.

Have a list fresh in mind of things you *don't* like about them. Write it down so you won't forget. Maybe the partnership has been together for a few years and it is going nowhere. It's not like being married, and it shouldn't be too difficult to adjust. No, the main chore is breaking the news. Be simple, just say you're sorry, but that it is over. Remind yourself that you just want to be happy.

Many relationships are never meant to be. How we get into these situations is a mystery; they just happen. It could all be attributed to "timing and circumstance." The initial meeting came at a time you were feeling lonely. Perhaps you had just broken up with someone, a best friend had moved, or a family member passed away. Sadness and loneliness were close companions when someone came along and cheered you up. And they just happened to be rebounding from a similar experience. After meeting, then looking to each other for a remedy, suddenly you moved in together and were officially "involved." You are two different people. The relationship hasn't the slightest chance of enduring the test of time. Both have had enough time together to know you're wrong for each other. It's what's called a "strangling relationship." You have been "enduring" this bond with the wrong person. They might even realize it too, but perhaps are willing to hang on. You're unhappy and ready to go on separately. Be strong and face the facts. State clearly where you stand.

ON THE ROAD TO FORGETTING

How do you achieve forgetfulness once the speech has been made? It should be reasonably easy, as you are the one who has decided upon a plan of action after the breakup. What about the partner? Theirs is the major adjustment, even though they might not have been happy either. Without plans other than to remain in that same quagmire of a relationship, they'll have it hard, while you were bright enough to recognize and strong enough to end the situation. Well, much of the same applies to both.

First of all, if the relationship has been one of a few years, most friends will be mutual. This poses a problem because many places you go will be filled with those who knew you both. Sometimes friends will forget and accidentally mention your former partner. Or maybe on occasion you might encounter "the ex" at a familiar haunt. These things make it difficult to forget quickly.

Napoleon was once to have said, "The greatest victory over a lost love . . . is flight!" I agree with ole-hand-in-the-coat. Get away! Go off on vacation and be around other singles who are laughing and having fun. If a vacation isn't affordable, go spend some time with friends in another part of town. Or, if possible, relocate and realize you are turning the pages to another chapter in life. Take old photographs and either burn them, send them back to your former roomie, or hide them deep in a box at the back of a closet. Do not sit home and feel sorry for yourself. Get out, meet people, and do things. You might be alone now, but you're better off. Convince yourself of that.

Think of the bad times shared and look forward to good times with someone else. Think of ridiculous things that turned you off, but you let slide because you were in love. Convince yourself you are no longer in love. Evaluate pluses and minuses of the relationship. If half the times were happy and the other half unhappy, the total is *zero* — nothing! Talk to friends and ask them never to mention so-and-so's name again.

A few years back my romance of over three years ended. It wasn't a case of anyone cheating or the result of a big quarrel; it was just that we both realized we were at a standstill and it was time the alliance ended. Trouble was, *she* ended it. Can you believe that? I was waiting for the right time to spring my plans to split on her, but *she did it first!* How could she do such a thing?

Now, isn't that what most women would term "typically male"? Your ego gets flattened. If it was our ego only that was injured, perhaps we weren't in love after all. Maybe like most people in those no-win situations, we were in a *habit*, each trying to hang on for a few days, a few weeks, a few months or (egads!) a few *years* longer. It happens every day because we take the easy way. We avoid change, being afraid to go out and search again. Don't be afraid; be happy. You're free! You were bright enough to recognize your plight and strong enough to do something about it. You are about to embark upon a new adventure. In the meantime, there will be a mourning period due to a fear of being alone. Yeah, it happened to me this time, but I was determined to shorten the adjustment period.

Different routes bypassed some of the restaurants we had frequented. Switching radio stations helped avoid songs reminding me of her. Her name came out of my address book. I found myself hurting inside, missing her terribly, and wishing she'd come back through the door just one more time. I stayed home for a few days, hoping the phone would ring. Yes, she was gone. What to do? I didn't feel like doing anything, but knew life wasn't over — maybe just saddened for a while. Reality had to be faced.

Five days passed. I had been locked in my apartment feeling lonely and sorry for myself, even though she wasn't right for me. Then memories of the bad parts of our relationship began to come: the many times we were unhappy, when we argued, how often I stormed out of the room. There were times when we were angry and actually disliked each other. Determined not to burden my friends with my problems any longer, I felt strong enough to handle it.

After showering, shaving, and putting on a sporty outfit, I went out to "hunt," to meet someone new to help take my mind off of her. The car started right up, I pulled the lever to reverse, then turned the engine off and went back upstairs to my condo. It was time to undress, put on pajamas, plunk some popcorn in the microwave, open a can of diet soda, and let Johnny cheer me up. I happened to catch his opening monologue but couldn't hear any of the words. Poor me . . . wounded and alone. Suddenly, awakening to find the Carson show over, I was knee-deep in Letterman. The guest at the moment didn't fill the void, so off went the TV, and on to bed. I lay back, eyes wide open, and began to suffer.

It takes determination to get yourself into action. When starting that engine and backing up, turn the wheel and drive out. Stop at the first place that has some semblance of life and rush in. Order something to eat or drink, look around to see the people, and ask one of the other alone people to dance. Yes, get around others. And, if you are fortunate enough to meet someone who is cordial, do not lay your problems on them. Be happy, positive, and as cheerful as your broken heart will allow. Try to enjoy yourself and forget all the grief.

Yes, *force* yourself to go places. Do new things, even if you think they won't be fun. You'll be surprised how many *are* fun. Be determined to remember this person was not for you. Think highly of yourself and imagine how lucky that neat-looking individual over there would be if he or she could get you. Feel confident and smile. Determine what you're after. If it's someone to just talk to and have a late breakfast with, make your play. State your case, and chances are you'll find many takers.

However, play it cool; don't look overanxious or desperate. All you want is someone — anyone — just to talk to, to help ease this loneliness. I'm not suggesting you attempt a "roll in the hay" with the first willing prospect. Don't look for love so soon after the breakup, as you might be rebounding and could choose incorrectly again. You are not desperate, for goodness' sakes. It's just a change, so welcome that change. We all agree it's for the better.

Look yourself over in the mirror. Not bad, huh? In fact, pretty darn good, right? Force yourself to smile and laugh, even if you feel like crying. Do not wallow in self-pity. If you stay home, I promise there will be a scarcity of folks knocking on your door, asking if you just broke up and are available. Go out there and seek — maybe advertise.

When alone, thoughts of your "ex" will pop into your mind if you allow it. When this happens, imagine them in an awful situation. Think of the times they were moody and made you miserable. Remember things they did that secretly turned you off. Realize you never would have been completely happy. There were too many obstacles. Look at how fat her mother is. Will she be that fat too? She looks just like her mother. Or think of his father; that pot belly and bald head. He is starting to get more of a "widow's peak" than he should at this age. He'll probably be just like his father. Ugh! Continue picturing these awful things to help erase "them" from your mind. Know that your life has changed, but it must go on. In the meantime, imagine how wonderful your next someone could be and how well you could both get along. Fantasize and plan!

Refrain from watching love stories on television or reading books involving romance. It will just cause more pain. And expect to hear more stories about your former partner than you ever dreamed existed. A mutual friend might let you in on a secret. "Did you know what's-their-name started seeing an ex-lover the last six months you two were together?"

That will cause both hurt and anger. Why in the *hell* didn't they tell you about that a long time ago, so you wouldn't have remained in that unpleasant situation so long?

Also, be prepared for their friends hitting on you — both unmarried *and* married ones. In fact, avoid those old friends for a while because they just can't help mentioning what's-their-name now and then.

Maybe you can relocate to another part of town. If living in an apartment, why not move? Those who live in a house perhaps could buy some new furniture or rearrange the old. *Anything* to change the looks of what was. Think about a shopping spree. Spoil yourself. Get one of those charge cards and squander a bit. Buy frivolous and fun things, even if you might wear them only a few times. Try to change your image with those new clothes, and maybe you can buy things *you* like since you don't have to please, appease, or account to anyone anymore.

Oh, you're wondering about the conclusion of my story? Well, after four nights "on the prowl" I met a girl who had just moved into the city. She didn't know anyone and was nervous about sitting in the club, at the bar, alone. I sat next to her and we began to talk. We left the club, had dinner at a quiet little French cafe, and became friends and saw each other quite often over a period of the next month or so. She helped nurse me out of my sadness and bring new ideas into my life, while making me realize there are a lot of people out there searching for happiness, and the only way to find them is to look for them.

The memory of my past love faded and within a few months, it was possible to look back and see it never should have been. We all do that, don't we? We feel as though our world is going to end without "them." Then, when forced to be without them and meet someone new, we could kick ourselves for wasting so much time on a relationship that was bordering on the absurd.

A few years have passed and she is but another photograph in my book of life. Yes, I took some of her best shots from that box in the closet and put them in my large collection book. I can look at her now and remember the good times and not feel any pain or remorse. We're both married — to other people. Hopefully, we will stay married to our present mates. The story ends well. We are, since I last talked to her, contented in our new lives with our new partners.

DON'T OVERINDULGE OR OVERREACT

What about *sex*? We've managed to sidestep that word throughout most of this text. Many psychologists agree that sex, though a temporary release, could be damaging, certainly not as fulfilling, as when this transition period ends. It isn't necessary to test your attractiveness by experimenting with various partners. Just *meet* new people, find out what's been going on in the world while you've been hibernating in a "going nowhere" involvement. Too often, "alone" people resort to overeating, or alcohol or drugs. And what does that accomplish? It only compounds problems.

Before going to a great expense of any kind and before making some tragic error in judgment, *do* read through this book. There are so many examples and stories and many of these you can relate to and identify with to help you understand and ease your pain.

I once had a friend who was constantly in love. Whether he was truly in love or not wasn't important; it only mattered that he *thought* he was. When his love affairs ended, he would go into mourning. Sometimes these periods would last for a few days, but more often for a few weeks. His life was a continuing soap opera, a series of ups and downs. Whether he was a manic-depressive or not, we never determined. But he certainly had all the signs.

He would meet a girl and come on strong; you know, tell

her the things he was certain she wanted to hear, and take her to the right places. He would slip into a role and actually *be* the person he felt she wanted. Within three or four splendid dates, the real him would emerge and his new friend would realize he was a totally different person. She would end the relationship, and my friend would go through these repeated periods of paniful suffering.

He wasn't certain he truly felt anything for these girls. After having the same scenario repeat itself many times, he decided to seek professional help. Some real mind-digging was needed and only a psychiatrist was equipped to supply it. After several months of therapy, my friend learned he was unsure of himself. He lacked self-confidence. He felt certain he wasn't good enough for anyone, so he became someone else. Many people could have been caught up in a situation with someone like this who wasn't truly responsible for his actions. If you have known people like this, try to understand them, and forgive them. They're no good either to you or themselves until they have been helped. My friend is now married and has been for five years. Everything seems to be just fine.

WITH EXPERIENCE COMES WISDOM

If you have felt trapped with someone pretending to be what they really weren't, trying to manipulate you, leading you through *their* day the way *they* like it, it should be easy to forget them. Learn how to *avoid* a potential unhappy relationship before it begins — *before* you have to plan on how to get out of it and forget them.

As we grow older, understanding tends to increase. Tolerance decreases. Most of us get smarter and learn from our experiences. Looking back on past relationships that ended and comparing them to this present relationship that *should* end, lets us know that we *will* survive. It's easy to tell a person *what* to do, but much more difficult to *do* it. I am evidence of that. I've lived it all.

There are many books dedicated solely to forgetting someone. The subject is important to the lives of so many that it is necessary to go into great detail in order to offer a solution. This chapter will help many. Studying breakup, divorce, a mate cheating, or how to find someone who will take up this lonely spot in your life is certainly essential to your happiness. The entire book solves the majority of these problems.

Chapter Seven

How to Attract a New Love

If you haven't been able to find someone with whom to share life, and maybe it's been a while since you've enjoyed a satisfying relationship, then it's time to make some adjustments. Let's begin by looking in the mirror. Feel something about you is unattractive? Why not see what changes could possibly be made? Chapter 1 deals with *The Physical You* and presents several avenues from which to choose. Let's suppose you've already made those modifications, yet the situation remains the same — alone and lonely. Take a closer look in the mirror. What's really there? What about your expression? Is it unhappy, tired, stressed, or desperate? Do you feel depressed, out of sorts, or maybe just plain ordinary? Maybe others tend to focus on these negative qualities too.

Then we have to further explore several other areas of character. Perhaps there's a need to work on attitude, sense of humor, confidence, outlook on life, behavior, speech, style or social graces. Everything is important when "out there" trying to meet someone. Could it be that areas of your personality need polishing? Perhaps all the right qualities are there, but you're just timid or unsure of how to use them to the best advantage.

Are you able to interact with others? This is probably the first step in getting to know someone: *communication.* Are you a good conversationalist, or do people think of you as a bit dull or boring? Notice that those who tend to attract the most attention initially are people who have interesting things to say. It's not necessary to go on a safari or become an astronaut to be fascinating. Being a near-authority on almost any subject, or even being enthusiastic regarding several others, will easily captivate listeners.

There are many interesting things to talk about. An unusual profession could stimulate others by sharing various points of inside information. Possibly, a hobby is interesting to many, or unique ideas on how to solve everyday problems can provide subjects. In the beginning, it might be useful to read more about world events or politics. Current events often initiate passionate discussions. Develop opinions and be ready to interject timely comments or quote the views of others.

Yes, this should be an excellent beginning if communication is an area of weakness. While developing various areas of knowledge, be especially attentive to others. Look around and analyze others in the crowd. Listen to what people are saying and how they project themselves. Expect to pick up some tips from their conversations. Then go home and practice in front of a mirror or into a tape recorder. Build up confidence and really begin developing a great personality.

I recall reading about a very famous Italian playboy of the 1950s, Porfirio Rubirosa, who was always in demand by the wealthiest of women. He was attractive, not especially in a physical way, but by having a way of making people feel unique and important. He had charisma. He spoke several languages and developed many interests, one of which was polo. Actually, Porfirio was far from handsome, with a rather large nose and an equally large set of ears. Still, the most beautiful and desirable women in the world pursued him fervently. Why? Because he knew how to carry on a conversation even with an heiress. "Your gown is lovely, my dear, it brings out the natural blossom in your cheeks." Ha! Think *anyone* wouldn't like to hear a compliment like that? "And your jewels, not only are they exquisite, but they accent your eyes perfectly. Do tell me about them." Yes, Porfirio knew how to play "the game."

If you're not quite sure what to say, turn the tables around and talk about the other person. Ask about *them*; give *them* the opportunity to relate to you about themselves. Most will relish the chance. This is a good technique even if you're shy. A degree of shyness can be alluring, but shyness to the point of being frightened is never going to work. Anything that inhibits the ability to speak or laugh, or simply to be yourself, must be changed. Shyness is often interpreted by many as a lack of self-confidence. Those not capable of forcing themselves into action should enlist the help of friends. Remember the saying, "If you don't take a chance, you'll never have a chance"? Well, it certainly does contain much truth.

Some overcompensate by concealing shyness and insecurities with overt aggression. They come on strong and never let up, virtually sending friends and potential admirers running in the opposite direction. Few of these people are alone, but they are often lonely. At first glance these overzealous extroverts may seem confident and secure. Then, at closer inspection, they seem nervous, too eager, loud, and persistent. Do you tend to duplicate these qualities, finding yourself overpowering others with your personality?

I had a friend one time, let's call him Doug, who had a different girl every time I saw him. Doug was the envy of many guys, since he always had a terrific-looking girl on his arm. After several months and years of seeing Doug with so many different women, I discovered he was lonely. I couldn't believe it, but it was true. So much time was spent selling himself, so much time winning them over, he never gave the relationships an opportunity to mature.

Give yourself and others time to share feelings and grow emotionally close. Finding a spouse isn't a race, although some people tend to treat it as such. A mutually satisfying relationship is what you want. Try to *be* that special person in someone else's life. Attaining all the "right" attitudes and "social graces" won't help people who are not genuinely satisfied with themselves. Open your eyes and see clearly, maybe for the first time. Discover who *you* really are and give others a chance to get to know that wonderful individual.

There are those who discard many could-be relationships for uncertain reasons. Disappointed in a past romance? Did you give them a chance? Involved with the wrong type? Were you disguising the "real you" in order to impress a barely known person? Start each new person at 100 percent. Start not only them at the top of the list, but yourself also. Be cautious, but don't be difficult. Don't make it necessary for them to *prove* themselves. Give them a chance to show they are worthy of your time, affection, and love.

APPEARANCE MATTERS

Along with your manner, attitude, and behavior, perhaps one of the most obvious things is your personal hygiene. It may seem silly to discuss something we all take for granted, but it's surprising how many people assume it's not that important. Ever noticed a good-looking man or woman you've been trying to meet and, when you finally got the opportunity to introduce yourself, you noticed their fingernails were dirty or they had an offensive odor? God forbid anyone should ever notice things like that about you!

We've all seen women in public with rollers in their hair or undergarments showing. Or men with greasy hair or an unshaven face. Of course, sometimes, due to unfortunate circumstances, we are forced to appear in public less than well-groomed. But how about usually? Do you take care to wash your face, wear make-up, and don neat, pressed clothing? Do you smell nice? Is your hair clean and styled in an attractive manner? Would you feel comfortable meeting a new someone as you look now? Don't expect to attract someone by looking just "presentable." There's a lot of competition out there and not one single reason to miss an opportunity.

FORTUNE AND FAME CAN'T HURT

To really attract someone fast, have *money*! Yep, go out and work your butt off to get a lot of money, because I don't think *anything* will attract someone faster. Of course, money alone doesn't buy happiness (although it makes misery *easy* to endure). And money alone is not sufficient. Some rich people are alone, lonely, and unhappy too.

We've all seen a nice-looking guy wearing Levi's and a T-shirt drive up in an old car. Many gals look and smile and maybe think it *might* be fun to meet him. *But,* let that same guy drive up in a Mercedes or a Porsche, one of those red jobbies that is mirror-shined. *Then* that guy is *gorgeous*! Right? And you *have* to meet him or you'll die!

Some years back I was introduced to a girl at a party in New York who was an heiress of one of the large steel fortunes in Europe. Not only was she rich, but she was outrageously beautiful with a delicate foreign accent. I *knew* it! I had died and gone to heaven . . . spellbound over all of "this" in one package. We made plans for dinner the following night. There was no sleep that night — just lying awake thinking, planning, *scheming* over this gorgeous, *rich* girl with an accent. Sure, she would have been attractive with her beauty alone, but the fact that she was an heiress was icing on the already tempting cake.

Yes, unfortunately, money *is* a certain way to attract someone. If you have a rotten personality, even if you are a bore, money will cause many to linger and put up with all sorts of crap — especially if the one enduring this slob is not accustomed to the finer things in life. If *both* are rich, then the relationship will last only as long as the two are compatible. Somewhere along the line of discontent, the poor person who was so attracted to the wealthy one will realize it is simply not worth the effort and unhappiness. He or she will either find someone else with money who is easier to get along with, or someone with no money who is an enjoyable person.

Try being *famous*! Brilliant surgeons, scientists, top professional athletes, entertainers, movie stars certainly attract others. As a kid growing up in a less-than-middle-class home, I determined to be rich someday. The only examples at the time were prizefighters. I decided to become an accomplished athlete and earn lots of cash. Also reasoning that smart people were wealthy, I decided I would try to become smart. I worked out daily with a punching bag and weights. I read as many books on different subjects as possible. I studied poetry and learned to play chess, meanwhile making myself a promise that if I couldn't punch or run or bat myself into riches, I would earn it with my brains.

Yes, even as a budding teenager, I was making plans for my future. Of course, not all of my plans worked out, but most of them did. I knew, even then, that in order to attract someone I had to develop interests and talents to make myself interesting.

This is where to stop and take a true self-appraisal. No matter what your age, it is *not* too late to develop talents and new interests and to become captivating. The more talents one has, the greater the chance of increasing the odds, and the bigger the likelihood of attracting someone whom you can enjoy. It's the same with a good education. It doesn't guarantee success or wealth, but it does give you more chips when you come up to the table to roll the dice.

NOW, GO OUT AND GET BUSY!

Let's assume you have corrected some weaker points and are ready to go out and attract someone. *Believe* that having self-confidence is the main factor in being able to attract the opposite sex. Ready, huh? You've got some neat clothes, smell good, have a few subjects to discuss, and your confidence is at an all-time high.

Go into a public place. It could be a party, club, or meeting. The first thing to do is make eye contact with someone. You're a girl. A guy is looking at you. His eyes show he is interested and you are also interested. What to do now? Look *back* at him, silly. Show a faint smile around your lips and drop those eyelids a tad, then turn away. In a moment or two, look back and he will be watching. Bet on it! This is when you show even a wider smile, maybe nod your head. Not a word has been spoken and there are thirty or more feet between you, but eye contact has given him the courage to rise from his seat and come over to talk. There are so many ways to attract someone, but be prepared to be able to hold onto that someone if you so desire. That's the reason for the emphasis on looking good and having a choice of several subjects to discuss.

You're a guy who walks into a party. After being introduced around by the hostess, you immediately have designs on two or three of the women present. Look at the way some look back. Also, at the way they might stand. Body language comes into play often and will give you the "go-ahead" to make the next move. If she tosses her head to one side or seems to preen her hair while she glances your way, get the message. She might arch her back just a tad to show off those magnificent breasts you're already aware of. Or, she might purse her lips a bit in a sort of pout. She knows you're watching and is giving you the "green light." Stomp on that accelerator and drive on over.

Yeah, guys, women rule it all. Don't ever think otherwise.

When they make a move, you are trapped. The showing of that tantalizing pout on their lips leads a man forward blindly like a Tom to catnip. When they cross or uncross their legs in a certain way, there's a message being sent. When being introduced, notice the way they grasp your hand, or the way they turn their face or arch their pelvis in a "come hither" stance. You've had it, buddy. You've not only used knowledge to recognize these moves, but are ready to talk about anything to further arouse their interest. You are on your way to *not* being lonely.

It might seem like a big game to you . . . and it is! Maybe everything in life is a game, a competing for something or someone, and the more you know the *rules*, the closer you'll be to finding companionship. Most of all, with an awareness of what these various "game maneuvers" are, you'll be more likely to find that someone with whom to share happiness. Just remember the basics: *look* good, *smell* good, and *act* good. Remember attitude: be positive and have self-confidence. Smile! Have fun and and be ready to enjoy whatever comes up. Make that new person feel as if he or she is about to embark on a friendship or an adventure with a happy, fun-loving person. You've read what others have done, you've looked yourself over in the mirror, practiced self-improvement, and have adapted the necessary qualities. Now, go out and *attract someone!*

Chapter Eight

What to Look For in a Mate

I advise young people (and the not-so-young) to deal with choosing a mate *academically* as well as from the heart. Too often people marry the "wrong" person because they didn't make a list of what they wanted and what they knew, deep in their hearts, they could never accept.

Everybody seems interested in a list of what other people want and actually jump with glee while making their own list. It really is fun and can also be very rewarding. At best, you'll have a chance at a perfect mate, and at the least, you'll be able to go through hundreds like a "hot knife through butter." Yeah, you won't waste a lot of time on those who do not fit satisfactorily the qualifications you have set forth for yourself.

Prior to seeking a new love, we must make certain we are over or almost over the old one. Chapters 2, 3, and 6 give you pointers on how to forget someone. This chapter tells you, in no uncertain terms, what to look for.

First, let's give this new prospective companion a clean start. It's totally unfair to attempt involvement with someone new while still experiencing hurt or heartbreak, or wishing your former love were back.

OK. Here is the list, not necessarily in order of importance.

1. LOOKS
2. INTELLIGENCE
3. LOYALTY
4. COMPATIBILITY
5. SEX
6. ATTITUDE and SENSE OF HUMOR
7. SECURITY

Those seven "commandments" tell it all. Discussing each one can also help determine what's important to you. No, it isn't necessary to get a pencil and paper now, but after finishing the chapter, *make your list*! Use the following checklists for your convenience. Remember this is *your* happiness and *your* future! After giving these items some thought, you will probably be able to add other qualities to look for, things that are personally important.

1. LOOKS: This, as plastic as it is, was the *first* choice with men in choosing a mate. They wanted a girl who was good-looking. Thank goodness tastes differ because there are only so many 10s in the world. And who are these men anyway? Most of them wouldn't score 5 in *any* contest!

I'd like each of you to know that being with a beautiful (or handsome) person who is shallow is not nearly as satisfying as being with the person of "inner" beauty. Oh, I know, "Beauty is only skin deep whereas ugliness cuts clean to the bone." Cute saying that is cruel but also factual. My suggestion is to go over the entire list of prerequisites. There are several virtues that make people happy and compatible. It's amazing, once you get to know a person, how beautiful (or ugly) they can become once you know their inner traits.

For men *and* women, people will only think as much

about you as you think about yourself. You are usually treated the way you *demand* to be treated. If appearance is a major priority, know that the "inside" person is far more the smart choice than simply the one on the outside.

2. INTELLIGENCE: A major priority among the educated. Those who want intelligence will *not* be able to enjoy a mate simply because they are great to look at *if* there is no line of communication. An education (or lack of) can be detrimental, a case where opposites, usually, do *not* attract. After the dinner party or meeting, after the lovemaking, when the two of you are alone, there simply *must* be communication. What do you talk about? How can you explain anything or reach an agreement if your partner is not capable of discussing things on your level? If you're bright, I suggest you look for a bright partner. If you consider yourself a dunce, try to gain self-esteem.

Men are often intimidated by bright women. Don't be! Learn to accept and respect the fact that women are just as bright in most areas . . . if not brighter. Women want to be recognized for more than their beauty. I've always enjoyed being around a person brighter than I; you can learn from each other.

There are statistics on couples who are happily together with varying intelligence levels, but not huge gaps. So look at it all! Never discard a potentially wonderful person who doesn't exactly measure up. I advocate moderation.

3. LOYALTY: Wow! What an important prerequisite this is! Some people want truth. Personally, I think *loyalty* triumphs over *truth* any day of the week. Truth simply could mean one partner has an affair with the grocery boy, butler, his best friend (or the babysitter, maid, and *her* best friend) and the other partner found out all that has been going on because the guilty party is *truthful*. Whereas, with loyalty, there is nothing to tell.

How miserable are those travelers who try to call their

mates and receive no answer. Some try several times during an evening and still no answer, even until the wee hours of the morning when there was no reason for the loved ones not to be home. If loyalty exists in the relationship, the answer could be the phone was out of order or perhaps unplugged. But without that built-in confidence, that out-of-town person could go crazy in just a few short hours.

Loyalty is a prime factor to being happy. Being able to trust someone satisfies the mind and the heart. No need to suffer, wondering what the partner is up to. How nice it is to know they are loyal.

4. COMPATIBILITY: This doesn't mean enjoying doing *all* things together, but it helps to enjoy doing most things together. It isn't necessary to adore doing everything your mate does, but one cannot *hate* something *they* love. Of course, every person is an individual, and there is no such thing as a perfect match. For instance, does he have a passion for bowling and wants to drag you along at every opportunity? You love him, but bowling, you feel, brings out the Neanderthal in most men and you would prefer taking a language class or visiting the museum. Then do it! Schedule those activities he doesn't care anything about while he is enjoying his favorite pastime. Then, during other free times, both can appreciate mutual outings without conflict. Simple? Who said you had to be attached at the hip to be a happy couple?

In many cases, compromise is the only solution when opposites attract. One girlfriend loved rock and roll music all the time. My preference was easy-listening music on the stereo. I remember dancing to Dean Martin and Johnny Mathis (and still enjoy hearing those memorable love songs), while she preferred songs devoid of words and comprising irregular noises, shrieks, and grunts. But there were so many other things we enjoyed together we eventually worked it out. I would go shake and vibrate a few times each month and she, in turn, agreed to ease into my "slow dances" as often. Yes, with compromise, one can learn new avenues of fun. After a while she would sometimes even suggest slow music, and I even found myself tapping my foot to some of her less raucous rock and roll tunes.

I interviewed many people who were over sixty years old. Their list of prerequisites was not as extensive as the lists I have in this book. All they truly wanted in a mate was someone who was compatible and someone with whom they could share companionship. Think about this for a moment and see if these two prerequisites might take in *everything!* I feel they are excellent guidelines for people of all ages.

5. SEX: Sex is near the end of my list, but that doesn't necessarily mean it will *remain* at the end. Sex certainly *is* important, but there must be other ingredients present before sex can be appreciated to the fullest. How nice it is to hold someone and truly want to be close to them, as close as you can get. How wonderful it is to laugh with them and share some of their little secrets and to have feelings for them as a person as well as a sex partner. How fulfilling it is to enjoy being with a person before, during, and *after* sex.

Sex is the big "traveler" on this list of prerequisites, climbing and falling during an extended relationship. It might be "the" thing tonight, whereas, a year from now it becomes simply "a" thing. However, if sex is not good at the beginning, when the fire and passion and newness is present, it probably has little chance to last as a commitment progresses. In some instances it can, but in most cases, no way! And that is fact! Ask any married couple; ask your neighbor or best friend. Ask yourself!

Many of those I interviewed who had been married a dozen or more years made a joke about sex. "Making love to the same person over and over again is like scratching a place that doesn't itch anymore!" Funny saying, but sadly a universal feeling with most marrieds — unless, of course, the persons together for this extended period of time *make* it interesting.

At the beginning of a relationship, hormones are whirling around in each person's body and they are excited and "always ready." As time passes, it isn't as exciting because it is no longer new. There are books out that tell you, in explicit detail, some of the things you both can do to change the joke into an outright lie. I have a close friend, Bob Schwartz, a best-selling author who wrote a book titled *The One-Hour Orgasm*. Don't scoff at the title *or* the contents. The information in this book has brought a renewed sex life to thousands.

Please don't be misled by satisfactory or wild sex at the beginning of a relationship. The learned call this beginning love "passionate love." As time passes, a "together-love" is termed "companionate love" — a less wild form. It is *still* possible for passionate love at *any* age and regardless how long two people have been together. But it doesn't just happen — it has to be learned and practiced. If partners are considerate of each other's feelings, wants, and needs, and if they practice keeping the intensity of that spark alive, the passion does not have to wane.

6. ATTITUDE and SENSE OF HUMOR: Most women responding to my five-year survey put this quality at the top of their list. It's important to many men, also. The way women treat others and how they respond to unpleasant circumstances has a direct effect on the way most men act in a similar situation. How wonderful it is to wake up in the morning next to someone who has a smiling face and first words that are cheerful.

There are many trials and tribulations in a relationship, as well as in everyday life. It is not only *important* to have a sense of humor; it is *necessary* for survival in many instances. How often so-called crises, pitfalls, and situations are thrust before us to deal with when we least expect them, or when we cannot seem to cope. A sense of humor alleviates tension and makes those enormous problems almost amusing and controllable. We all love to be around someone who can make us laugh and forget our woes.

Armed with a good attitude, it's possible to go one-on-one against the world and win! Why get upset over life's little annoyances or complain to everyone about petty problems? It's depressing to be in a good mood and come home to find your mate irritable or annoyed over something trivial to most. It might seem a deliberate attempt to dissipate your elevated feelings instead of trying to work out a solution and maintain the harmony you enjoy after a hard day's work. Choose someone usually happy and contented, who complements your natural good nature.

7. SECURITY: When talking about "security," we mean not only dollar signs, but whether that person will support you in all ways. Will they be there in times of strife or hardship? What about helping hold the household together if you lose your job? Can they readily adjust to a new city if you are promoted and transferred to a new position? Is your chosen one supportive of your goals and ready to offer strength when you are emotionally spent? Other than these major things, can you depend on your partner to help out on a moment's notice? Would they consider changing personal plans in order to cover for you if necessary? Do you make your partner feel secure? Would you also "be there" whenever needed, even if it was inconvenient?

Security also means the ability to share equally in the responsibility of financial safety. Lifestyle and needs have bearing on every situation. Is your spouse willing to trim luxuries in order to provide a nest egg for the future, for the family? Know that money certainly is important in a relationship and worthy of consideration. It is unquestionably one of the main reasons for not remaining together. Would it be fair to say: "A marriage between two rich people is a merger; a marriage between two poor people, a *disaster*; but a marriage between someone rich and someone poor possibly terrific?" Why *not*? If many of the other attributes on the list exist, contrary to popular belief, money really doesn't make that much difference . . . or shouldn't.

STARTING YOUR LIST

The above attributes and virtues are sufficient to promote an enduring relationship. Now, choose which are the important ones for you. Someone has said, "There are two kinds of perfect people in the world: the kind we dream about, and the kind that don't exist." Too, how can we expect to find all the above qualities in someone if we cannot provide much in return? In fact, looking over the above seven makes me wonder which one to really put at the top of my list. While wanting someone physically attractive, I *demand* loyalty. A Rhodes Scholar isn't necessary, but I do need intelligence in my mate. Hopefully, we are compatible, but we don't have to do everything with the same amount of enthusiasm. Sex is still important, even in my autumn years. Attitude and sense of humor are certainly relaxing and comforting to one's soul, and I guess I could let financial security slide a bit with someone who backs me in decisions more often than not. We must determine which are important and add some of our own ingredients, putting them in a pot, stirring, and *academically* choosing our next companion. It will multiply chances for a successful relationship.

Now choose from my list of seven prerequisites and write them in the order best suiting *you*, making "1" the *most* important attribute. At least have a "plan." Do understand one thing: the person you choose must possess attributes in your most important areas but can be average in the insignificant ones. This chart should give an idea of how to make selections. Remember, don't expect someone to be all-everything.

I was conducting a seminar of divorced people in Chicago once and a lady from the crowd said, "Mr. Billac, my name is Marilyn and I'm fifty-three years old. I've been divorced three years and I'm looking for a man. He doesn't have to be the most handsome man alive but he must be distinguished-looking. I'd like him to be intelligent and have a great sense of humor. He must be rich, rich, rich, spoil me, and have sex whenever I ask. What do you think of that?"

I paused for a moment to think, then looked out into the audience at Marilyn, seated way in the back. "Marilyn," I said, "I'D MARRY HIM!"

Rarely will you get it all! But the important parts to you, I suggest you demand. Compromise in some of the lesser areas.

1.

2.

3.

4.

5.

6.

7.

Now add a list of *additional* virtues you'd like your mate to possess:

1.

2.

3.

4.

5.

6.

7.

Now review the previous lists and add qualifications of your particular potential companions to see how they match up to your expectations. Space is available for three. Go ahead, make the list! It's fun and just might open your eyes to what could be important for a successful relationship.

Name #1: _George B. Moore_

1.

2.

3.

4.

5.

6.

7.

8.

9.

10.

Name #2: _____

1.

2.

3.

4.
5.
6.
7.
8.
9.
10.

Name #3: _____

1.
2.
3.
4.
5.
6.
7.
8.
9.
10.

  This upcoming list is meant to be humorous but informative. In fact, even the humorous parts are quite accurate. You'll be able to identify some characteristics with past dates and maybe even with your present mate. It will be fun to share your list and compare it with those of your friends. You'll be surprised how much such a simple academic procedure will enlighten you on what to look for in a mate.

Why not circle the attributes you would like to have in a mate, as well as your more stringent demands? Then, when finding someone who might be important in your life, match their qualifications against the ones you've previously circled and marked. (The list is geared to a woman's preference, so revise accordingly if you are a man.)

LOOKS:

DEMANDS (3)	WOULD LIKE (2)	WILL ACCEPT (1)	LAST RESORT (−3)
Handsome	Good-looking	Average	Looks don't count
Tall	Almost tall	Short	"Tattoo"
Good body	Not big muscles	No muscles	Don Knotts similarity
Strong	Not weak	So-so	Wimp
Virile	Macho	Paunch	Jellyroll
Sexy	Attractive	Limited appeal	Toad

INTELLIGENCE:

Genius	Very smart	Kind of bright	Uneducated
Well-versed	Witty	Catches on	Dumb
Imaginative	Interesting	Amusing	Dull
Clever	Resourceful	Smooth	Slow
Charismatic	Appealing	Personable	Offensive

LOYALTY:

Loyal	Truthful	Tells white lies	No conscience
Faithful	Fantasizer	Lusts	Dog in heat
Generous	Giving	Shares	Scrooge
Sincere	Reliable	Honest	Deceitful
Honorable	Considerate	Dutiful	Tricky

COMPATIBILITY:

Attentive	Listener	Daydreamer	Dodo
Exciting	Enthusiastic	Avid	Tense
Romantic	Charming	Pleasant	Mushy
Creative	Bright	Productive	Lazy

SEX:
Always ready	<u>Eager</u>	Once a week	Grudgingly
Passionate	<u>Experimental</u>	Traditional	Indifferent
Sensual	<u>Sensitive</u>	Appreciative	Listless
<u>Well-groomed</u> 3	<u>Clean-shaven</u> 3	Slight stubble	Gross

ATTITUDE and SENSE OF HUMOR:
Playful	<u>Fun</u> 3	Prankster	Sadist
<u>Mischievous</u>	Impish	<u>Teases</u>	Taunts
<u>Spontaneous</u>	Impulsive	Rehearsed	Stupid
Confident	3<u>Well-adjusted</u>	Unsure	Defensive

SECURITY:
<u>Ambitious</u> 3	<u>Motivated</u> 3	Satisfied	Survives
Professional 3	<u>Businessman</u> 3	3Hard worker	Bum
Resourceful 3	<u>Leader</u> 3	3 <u>Good provider</u>	No ability
Successful 3	Thriving 3	3 Aware	Failing
Caring 3	<u>Concerned</u> 3	3Nice	Neglectful

That was fun, wasn't it? Did you learn anything from the chart? Are you now able to more clearly identify some of the attributes hoped for in a mate? Are some of the other qualities relative to previous beaus enabling you to focus more upon what to search for now? Remember, plan and practice to be able to actually change things. To be successful, be prepared to increase the chances of winning this war against loneliness. Let's stack the odds in your favor.

Go back over the chart and mark some columns for yourself, giving 3 points for something you demand, 2 for something you'd like, 1 for something you will accept and MINUS 3 as last resort. Higher scores indicate higher demands.

Do not take that last resort column unless it is the looks category. If they are rich, looks have a way of moving over to the demand side. Sad but true. Look around and see what I'm talking about.

The above list could show you what you *have*, what you *had*, or what you're *looking for*.

Now, go on to the next chapter and be prepared to make yet another list . . . of things you *cannot accept*. With all of this information, it should be fairly easy to choose someone with whom to enjoy life. It has worked for others, why not you?

Chapter Nine

Things You Cannot Accept

After making your list of what you want in a person, don't neglect to write down what you do *not* want. There are some sure signs in a relationship that can be detected early and easily. This is yet another reason never to rush into things. There's time. Take it easy; be slow and smart.

1. ALCOHOL: If your partner drinks too much, either get him to seek help or blow him off. Too often people get involved then learn they cannot accept the stress and erratic behavior of alcoholics. They are too loud and embarrassing at parties, disruptive and undependable at home. Drinking done in moderation is acceptable, but too much alcohol will tear people apart.

Many alcoholics become violent and don't know why. They hurt people both mentally and physically, then don't remember doing it. You'll remember it, though, and so will your scarred and battered children. Either the partner seeks help to combat this drinking, or it's time to leave. If the problem is there before you become involved, be aware that it could wreck a potentially good relationship.

2. NARCOTICS: There is no need to point out the wreck people have made of their lives and careers because of excessive use of drugs. Those who have conquered their addiction act as living testimonies to the harmful effects of drugs. Many are not alive to attest to anything. It begins innocently enough, just recreational drugs to relax and have fun. Soon, major priorities seem to be out of focus, and too much time and money is wasted on the wrong things. Before very long, a user needs professional help and not "understanding." Either they put it away, or it will put them away. Don't let narcotics, either through personal use or use by a loved one, affect your happiness. Drug users usually have no self-confidence. They kid themselves, feeling drugs are necessary for them to endure life. Life doesn't *have* to be endured — it can be enjoyed. Hopefully, the drug user will realize this in time and will abandon this harmful, often deadly habit.

3. VIOLENCE: People are violent for a number of reasons. If your mate draws his hand back at you one time, it's possible to forgive him and issue a warning that if it ever happens again, you're leaving. If he uncorks that hand, leave him immediately and suggest he get counseling *before* you agree to return.

People get violent over rejection, inadequacy, impotency, stress, drugs or alcohol, or they just might be plain "mean." Why should you care if his mother beat him or his daddy left him? This is *your* life, and his childhood should not be your responsibility. The world can be tough enough to live in without the fear of being physically abused for any reason.

A quick temper is a sickness; it isn't normal. The police lines are inundated with calls from battered wives and even a few battered husbands. And it doesn't necessarily stop with you. It happens to hundreds of thousands of children — babies even. If *you* want to be stupid and take this abuse, as a grownup it's your dumb choice. But please don't condemn your children to this mind- and body-damaging treatment. *Report them!* There are agencies and shelters and *the law* to protect you from this.

No, do not live in a turbulent environment. You and your family can easily find a more conducive atmosphere in which to live and be happy. Living on your own is ten times better than being with an abusive mate.

4. PHILANDERING: Let's face it. Some people are just born cheaters and only something very profound can change this. More often than not, there will be no such change unless they get caught. Then they'll swear on all that is sacred not to do it again, until you find that within a few weeks of forgiveness, it's happening again. Non-monogamy often is a pattern and not a one-time incident with most males (as opposed to females), recent studies indicate. Some casual flirting is acceptable and interpreted as "just being friendly." But out-and-out extramarital affairs should not, in this author's opinion, be tolerated.

Scoundrels — those accustomed to having more than one relationship at a time — can change. But play it smart and take time to see for yourself if there *is* a change. Many women are attracted to the "playboy" and rightly so, because these guys have all the pizzazz everyone enjoys. But when it comes time to choosing a lifelong companion, make certain you take time in that relationship before making a permanent decision.

5. GAMBLING: "All things," the wise old father of a friend of mine once told me, "should be done in moderation." He made this statement one Sunday afternoon when overhearing his son and me about to change a $50 bet to $500. "You guys can afford to lose the fifty, but don't you think five hundred dollars takes the fun out of the wager? Why not keep the fifty-dollar bet and enjoy the game?" He was right! We wanted to

change a fun bet to a serious one. We almost took the first step in becoming gamblers. We ended up losing only the fifty, but to this day I remember those wise words when I feel as though I am about to "slip" in some area.

Gambling is a disease. One friend stood up at the crap table for such an extended period of time, his wife would periodically squirt deodorant under his arms. It must have been a fun Las Vegas vacation for her, huh? I've known people who used their homes as collateral, and lost. Once, I met a couple who went to Las Vegas to get married. They lost all their money, then couldn't afford a preacher. The guy gambled too much, and the girl should have seen this weak side of him then. She didn't. I loaned them money for the preacher and license. Five years and two kids later, he is still wagering and they are getting a divorce.

Gambling can be as harmful as alcohol or narcotics and is just as addictive. If you understand your partner is a chronic gambler, know they will experience temporary victories, but the end result will be a broken heart, no funds, and the uncertainty as to whether you'll have a roof over your head the next day. I say *run!*

6. LYING: Everyone, for the most part, embellishes a favorite tale. But actual lying, either to cover an error or hurt someone else, is a no-no in a relationship. Many liars are experts. After all, anybody can tell the truth. But to tell a convincing lie you must be bright, have a good memory, and have no conscience when it comes to the outcome of that lie. It, too, is a disease and can be detrimental to a working relationship.

When I say "lie," I don't mean to confuse this with a "story teller." We've all heard a wife correct her husband when he was telling a story. For instance, this fellow was telling several other couples about taking fourteen and a half hours to clean the garage. The wife chimes in and says "Harold, it was only *fourteen* hours, dear." Then poor Harold tells of the time they drove fifty miles to find their dog who had run away from home. Wifey comes back with "Now, Harold, it wasn't *fifty* miles at all, it was only *forty-two* miles." You've witnessed such an incident, haven't you? Who really cares if it's half an hour or a couple of miles more or less? It has nothing at all to do with the story, but the wife wants to correct her husband as though he were a liar. The dog probably ran off to get away from his master's chiding wife. The next one to flee the scene might be Harold, searching for happiness with someone who will let him tell his stories uninterrupted.

Lies have caused unhappiness, divorce, and even death. They have ended partnerships, toppled governments, and caused as much pain as any dreaded disease. Chronic liars expect people not to believe them. A liar's true punishment is *they can never believe anyone else!*

7. LACK OF AMBITION: The sequence in which these "unacceptable" problem areas are positioned has no bearing on the order of their importance; they are *all* important. If your loved one has no ambition, then just realize you must settle for whatever happens in life, since your mate probably cannot help you morally, spiritually, or financially. There are many who are satisfied merely to exist. If you are not prepared to accept full responsibility for your future and that of your dependents, then maybe you should reconsider being with an uninspired partner. Because if you want "more," only a person with the motivation and willingness to reach out will make a suitable mate.

You can pretty well spot someone who has a future after being around him/her for a while. Sometimes, though, a person who has been striving for success for so many years will suddenly find the need to "get away from it all," and is willing to settle for less. Perhaps this person is only going through a temporary change and, after a short period of rest, will again resume his drive to "Make something of himself" and become successful. We all need time and a change of pace to regain our sanity. Perhaps with a little understanding your ambitious partner will soon be back on track.

8. TARDINESS: Not a big problem, but still a problem that deserves attention. If all humans would realize they have no *right* to steal another person's time, then maybe they would correct this malady. If you steal someone's wife, they might feel a loss but they can marry again. If you steal their money, they can earn more. But if you steal their *time*, it is not recoverable. Besides, it's always a real pain to have to wait for someone. It makes one uncomfortable, irritable and, again, it steals living. It's just no fun to have to break all speed records getting to the theater on time when your "friend" is always tardy. It's even less fun to have to race down the corridors of an airport and scratch on the doors of the plane hoping you won't miss your flight. Tardiness is an inconsiderate habit. Set one who is chronically tardy on the right track now!

9. RELIGION: I did my utmost to stay away from this subject. However, it is important to a successful relationship if one of the partners is of strong faith and the other shares this faith. Several dozen people interviewed said religion caused their romance to end. Some had strong religious convictions and did not make demands of their partner as long as they were allowed to practice their faith without objection or interference. Others managed to turn their passion off and bypass a partner who was not of the same faith. Rarely, during these interviews, was an agnostic or atheist paired with a husband or wife who held stringent religious values. The unmarried mixtures of believer and nonbeliever hadn't given their religious beliefs much thought. Nor had they given marriage much thought. Opposites do attract in many instances, but strong religious bonds coupled with those of lesser faith rarely work.

A friend of mine came home one day after a three-month

business venture abroad and found that his entire family had changed. While he was away, his wife, suffering from extreme desolation, succumbed to the influence of a new cult. In a few short weeks, she sold the cars and most of their possessions. The kids would no longer celebrate Christmas or birthdays. She and the family had been "saved." My buddy went berserk. His wife would not change her newfound beliefs. They divorced.

Then there was the marriage between two people of the same faith. They choose, through their religion, to do without many worldly goods and dedicate their lives to the Lord. They have children who are happy and they, too, live for the Lord. This is one of the nicest families I have ever met.

But even though religion is a powerful ingredient in holding many marriages together, it also can come between a relationship. If religion is strong in the life of your intended but not in yours, or vice versa, prepare for trouble ahead. Many religions simply forbid marrying someone who is not of the same faith.

10. GROSSLY OVERWEIGHT: These past few decades have intensified our desire toward achieving optimum health and physical fitness. Of course, you don't shop for a partner who is a hundred or more pounds over their ideal weight, but sometimes, due to worry, boredom, or half a dozen other excuses, the pounds accumulate and one day one could awaken to find a very large person in bed. An overweight mate is a flimsy reason to leave an otherwise stable relationship, but the weight could be endangering their health and they aren't quite as attractive as they used to be.

If you are currently involved in a health program because you find yourself growing in size, stick with it. Sometimes it is very discouraging to find your loved one thwarting your best efforts. Could there be any reason they might want to keep you looking fat and unattractive? Or perhaps you have reasons to insure your partner stays obese. Fat is a symptom of an underlying problem, whether it is emotional, mental, or physical. Try to uncover the real reason for those excess pounds. Your health, self-esteem, and the happiness of your mate are too important not to correct this problem.

11. CHRONICALLY UNEMPLOYED: We've all seen 'em! And for some reason the "boss" is always the one at fault. This certainly can be true once, maybe twice or even three times, but more often than not, the person who is always laid off or changing jobs is one who simply cannot follow the rules or get along with people, or both. Shy away from this guy. The only good thing about being a part of his life is that you'll make lots of friends standing in the soup line or at the unemployment office, getting those checks between jobs.

12. OVERLY CRITICAL: Ever notice the guy who is always ready with a "put down"? Usually, psychologists say, their feelings of inadequacy entice them to make you feel inadequate. That is the only way *they* can feel elevated. The trouble is, after a period of time, you have no self-esteem or confidence left. You begin to *believe* what they tell you. And that is exactly what you've been working so hard to get away from. Do not hang around anyone who makes you feel stupid, unattractive, or worthless. You deserve better than that.

We've all been guilty of this to a degree. It might begin as a mere joke. Soon it becomes a habit and you find yourself "putting down" the person you love in front of friends. Even if the targeted party laughs along with everyone else, remember that deep down they are feeling hurt. If she is a lousy cook, then either use the microwave, go out to dinner more, or spring for cooking lessons. No need to ridicule her weakness in front of strangers or friends.

13. WORKAHOLIC: Usually, this is someone to be admired and they certainly have their place on this earth. Ironically

enough, you will be the one to receive your Ph.D. in understanding because you might as well be alone. It will probably be a very comfortable world filled with every material need except the need to be able to enjoy a two-week vacation, camping trips with the kids, or friends over for weekends barbecues. Forget it! He's busy at work. It turns him on. That doesn't necessarily mean he's bored with you or family life or anyone; he just likes work. Even during time off, his favorite topic is work. Maybe you can adjust. But if not, go find someone who either inherited a lot of money or someone who makes time to share.

14. TV ZOMBIE: Psychologists say this is an ever-increasing form of addiction for many, almost in the category with alcohol, narcotics, or gambling. There are some people who cannot be dragged away from the set. They watch cartoons, the old movies, PTL, "I Love Lucy" reruns, and even a few of the soaps. Not to mention sports! You can run around unscrewing some tubes (if you've got an old set), but you can't do it to all the sets. He's got the big one in the living room, table model in the bedroom, a small black and white in the workshop, and now, even one plugged into the cigarette lighter in the car. It's tough to compete for this man's attention.

Work for some compromise. Possibly while dating you were both too busy to watch TV. But now, after several years of marriage, he comes home and flops in front of the tube until bedtime. He might not even notice this addiction until he looks in the mirror and sees two square-shaped, bloodshot eyes looking back at him.

And he's probably unaware of his "trigger finger" syndrome. Why is it that men seem to enjoy playing with that remote control more than women do? If you plan to watch TV with him, prepare yourself to view every sport invented. And he'll use that clicker to change channels during each commercial, sometimes missing some of the original show, maybe even the *end* of the show! That clicker was invented for men chiefly to aggravate their mates, I'm convinced.

If you aren't an ardent TV watcher, you'd best plan doing something else. Otherwise, you'll be spending a lot of "alone moments" while he is glued to the set.

15. UNTIDY: This guy just doesn't give a damn where he throws his clothes . . . wet towel on the bathroom floor after a bath, toothpaste tube with a white or multicolored worm poking out, whiskers in the washbasin, and on and on. He doesn't care about his looks either. His pants might have cuffs dragging the ground like he just jumped off the potato boat from Ireland. He is a slob. If you are a neat-nik, he will drive you insane with his habits.

Then there's the flip-side of that untidy record, my sister-in-law. My brother is having a glass of iced tea and watching TV. He gets up to go to the bathroom and when he comes back, not only is his tea gone, but it's thrown out, the glass washed and back in the kitchen cabinet. Or, while in the bathroom, he takes a bottle of mouthwash from the cabinet and proceeds to gargle. The towel around his waist comes loose and he bends to pick it up. When he reaches for the bottle to screw the cap back on, his wife has already put the cap on, wiped the bottle, and replaced it in the cabinet. She is so extreme about being clean it makes everyone uncomfortable. Upon mentioning it to my brother one day, he took me outside to look at his van. The inside looked like a trash war had been going on. It was the only way he "got back at her," by trashing out the only item to which he alone has access. The ashtray was stacked with butts; there were crumpled beer cans on the floor with wadded-up paper and half a sandwich from weeks before. He showed me the *only* key.

"When I get out of the van," he explained happily to me, "I lock it. Rita hates it, but she allows it. If she didn't, I'd go nuts with all that cleaning and polishing. But, brother," he

Things You Cannot Accept

continued, "she is a wonderful wife and mother, and I have learned to cope with that awful cleanliness fetish she has. This crappy-looking van is my act of defiance against her. We get along in every other way and I'm happy," he finished. What could I say?

16. JEALOUSY: Succumbing to "pangs" of jealousy or envy on occasion is, to say the least, very human. When you or your mate fall into a pattern of "critical" jealousy, though, there is a problem. Doubt, suspicion, and possessiveness are by-products of an insecure person. Accusations and mistrust initiate ill-will and destructive feelings toward each other. Jealousy can surely poison a relationship faster than almost anything else. If you or your mate suffer from this malady, only serious counseling can alleviate the root of the problem.

One couple interviewed had just won over a bout with jealousy. The woman was the guilty party in that her husband was so handsome she thought every woman in the world wanted him. The wife wasn't bad looking but he, she felt, overshadowed her looks. The son-of-a-gun *was* handsome and women *did* look at him for a third time when they passed. It kept her upset most of the time, and she made life miserable for the poor guy who had been fortunate enough to inherit a fine arrangement of genes. When he was but minutes late, she questioned him. When he turned his face to cough at a restaurant, she suspected him of making goo-goo eyes at someone else. This jealousy was making their lives miserable. He had to constantly explain and prove his love and devotion to his wife. They went to a psychologist who, after many months of teaching and listening, solved the problem for them. "Just get a divorce!" he finally shouted in practiced desperation. "You apparently don't love your husband enough to trust him, and he doesn't love you enough to scar up his face. You were attracted to him because of his good looks, weren't you? Well, now that you have him, be flattered when others admire him."

The husband began to reinforce his wife's positive feelings about herself by showing how attractive he thought she was and that, combined with a few new pointers from a beautician, made her feel more desirable and more confident too. The beautiful couple were admired by both sexes. The counselor had to get "down and dirty" to straighten them out. It seemed to have worked.

Whew! Sixteen "look fors" should be sufficient to start your list, but there are probably a hundred more you can think of. Make that list! Understand that the word *compromise* can stretch just so far, but also know you will have to accept many of these lesser-important foibles in a mate. Yes, we humans have a long list of frailties. Understand that you, too, have a list of considerable length. Compromise with many of the lesser quirks a person might have for the more important things you must have in order for a relationship to endure. If *they* don't have the important attributes you feel you need, then there are a few choices: (1) alter your way of thinking or try to change your partner; (2) merely overlook these problem areas; or (3) just bypass the one who seems to have an arsenal of things you cannot accept.

Nobody promised it would be easy. Why not make a *real* effort in your search for someone who might be a permanent part of your life? It's worth the effort. We must all go through a "trial and error" period with new people. Gosh, I don't want to take the fun out of love and romance and make it a mathematical problem. Just be absolutely certain to understand the fact that you must be armed with all the information available to be able to choose correctly. This will enable you to find someone with whom to be compatible and who will help you not to be lonely — ever again.

List here the negative things about your present or prospective companion(s).

Things You Cannot Accept

Name:_____

1.
2.
3.
4.
5.
6.
7.
8.
9.
10.

Name:_____

1.
2.
3.
4.
5.
6.
7.
8.

9.

10.

Name:_____

1.

2.

3.

4.

5.

6.

7.

8.

9.

10.

Please don't be *too* discouraged after looking over the flaws in the persons you listed until you've tallied them and scratched off the bad points you might be able to accept. If this person matters to you more than that of a casual acquaintance or a "steady," it isn't necessary to be too harsh on them. Try to enjoy the good points, and enjoy the person for the moment. Not everyone will be Mr. or Ms. Perfect.

But if you are seriously considering this person as a permanent companion, you simply must recognize these major flaws and correct or accept them *now!* Not only must the good points outweigh the bad, *one* flaw could outweigh all the rest, depending on what you like and/or can accept. You are the only one who can make the decision. You're aware, at least, what to look for, and you are not going blindly into a relationship.

That is yet another smart reason to make the list — and by all means, *make* that list. The only way to derive full benefit of this book is to make the lists, no matter how inconsequential they might seem to you. They are important steps to take in finding someone with whom you can be happy and *not* be lonely.

Chapter Ten

Where to Find a New Companion

This, of course, depends solely on the type of person you are. We've already determined your category: you are one of the "alone" people, a member of the "walking wounded." Having decided the mourning period is over, you are out to really hunt.

First, make a plan. Choose the type of person you're looking for and go to an area where this someone might be found. If you're a country-western type, hit the "tonks" where the most pick-up trucks are parked. Rednecks and cowboys are always ready for a new fling. Arty types can choose from half a dozen art shows, antique auctions, or benefit dances held almost any weekend. Like sports? There are tennis tournaments, golf, basketball, football, etc. If you are a thirty-year-old who just walked out of a five-year relationship with her married boss, drop in on a Little League game in some nice neighborhood. Chances are, other than the "mad mothers" who are intimidating the opposing team's coaches and umpires, a few of the single fathers are also there.

I have a friend named Brad. We are both the same age and like the opposite sex. One time I had moved back from out-of-state and Brad was recovering from a broken romance. The timing was right for us to plan together. We prepared our assignation with the female population in general while toning our muscles at the local health club, then met at his apartment one evening to finalize our assault tactics. While scanning the newspapers for any special shows, auctions or benefit dinners, we planned to pursue the sophisticated type. After checking each other's wardrobe, having our new cars professionally cleaned, readying our apartments so that everything was neat, and removing any "old love" photographs, we went out!

The first evening we began early at an art show. There certainly were some interesting-looking girls there and we casually and slyly hit on almost each one. Wrong approach! Maybe the panic look was too visible. Well, we didn't "score," but didn't actually "strike out" either. Brad managed to get us invited to a barbecue the following Sunday and I met a lady whose husband was in another part of the building looking at her preferred art. The lady thought her niece might like to meet me. Not bad for a two-hour visit, drinking free drinks, eating free hors d'oeuvres and seeing "beautiful people." When the two of us left the gallery, it was about eight in the evening. Those things start and end early. We then decided on dinner at one of the finer restaurants and chose a table near the ladies' room. This way, we had a chance of seeing almost every female in the place. There simply is no female who can last through a few cocktails and a two-hour dinner without making a trip to the powder room. We smiled at every gal who passed on the way in and on the way out. They all had dates. We finished our dinner and left. Our final effort was at the largest "in" club in town.

We arrived at this club around eleven, just when the place had filled up to the point that elbow-room was a rarity. While trying to see through the smoke and flashing lights, we shoved our way to a small spot and both managed to squeeze in at the bar. After ordering drinks, Brad scanned to the left as I moved my head like a slow lighthouse beam to the right. Then facing each other, I observed where he had been looking, and he scanned where I had been looking. We decided to zero in on one, or two, or three. One was talking so much we certainly couldn't get our pitch in. Another was puffing on her cigarette as though it was her last wish granted before execution. One who looked great from the back turned to face us and had eyes so close together that, even in the semilight, she could be mistaken for a cyclops.

Ah ha! I thought. There's one. She's alone, doesn't appear to be waiting for anyone, seems a bit snooty, looks kinda bright, maybe mid to late twenties. Think I'll make a move. Brad apparently had the same plan and we got stuck trying to squeeze through a space only large enough for one. I nodded to Brad in the girl's direction. "That girl?" Brad nodded. Being good friends, we had already made arrangements on what we would do if we met two girls, one pretty and the other not-so-pretty. We agreed to let the females choose. We would make our approach, not really centering our attention on either one of them, then let the girls excuse themselves to the powder room and discuss which one of us they would take. We also agreed not to "sharp shoot" each other by saying cute little cuts like: "Oh, Brad is a terrific guy. He's a gentleman, will take you interesting places and is fun to be with, but of course, if he ever scores with you he'll tell everybody in town. And, I don't think his herpes is active at this point."

So, Brad and I went to the men's room to flip for this one girl. We were friends, weren't we? Brad won the coin toss and went out to head for "Miss Available." Much to his dismay, someone else had zeroed in on her while we were deciding. Rule #1: If you see someone you like, get over there pronto. Things to say should come automatically. But speed in pouncing on your prey is essential.

Where to Find a New Companion

Well, these were some of our tactics. We danced the remainder of the night with different girls. We laughed, made no rash moves, and were on our way to playing the singles game. In just one eight-hour evening, we had three dates each for the coming week, plus that shoot'em-up barbecue, the nice art-lover's niece, and a few other social events. Yes, in just one evening of getting *exposure,* we were "in the game" again. Do you see how easy it is?

Two girls can also implement this search routine. Perhaps modify the plan of action to suit your needs. Make sure you and your friend are of near-equal caliber. Try to face the facts. Let's assume you're fairly attractive. Then, select a girlfriend who has qualities to complement your own. Set up some rules as Brad and I did, and begin the fun.

Let's say you go to a play. No matter what the play is about, select one with at least three acts, which means *two* intermissions. Purchase tickets in the first fifteen rows so your "prospect" will neither think you're broke, nor will he be on welfare (unless, of course, he is playing the same game). A near-the-front-row-seat is prime because everyone sees the two of you walk in. Wear a neat outfit, maybe basic black, but sexy. And accessorize with light jewelry, small purse, fine fur or a fancy cape that required at least three months in layaway. When walking down the aisle, don't put on a "searching" look — too obvious and too anxious. Casually move your head from side to side and hope some alone-guys are there to spot you. Enjoy the performance, but stick to your plan. Your purpose is, primarily, to find someone to halt loneliness. Just before the first intermission, get ready to spring up and hurriedly make way to the rear and to a position just across from the bar in the lobby. Don't hang out by the men's room; that's only for restaurants and clubs.

When you spot someone that looks eligible, move next to him and nudge his elbow. When he turns and smiles, look interested — not too eager, just "interested." If he turns out to have all his teeth missing when he smiles, move on to the next "candidate." Why not drop a glove? It's corny, of course, but it works. And all we're after is success, right?

When the horn sounds three short blasts, try to be almost the last one in. This gives a chance for that long stroll down the aisle to your seat and another grand entrance — a chance for some male prospect to see you. During the next intermission, do the same thing. Remember, get exposure and, if nothing happens, don't worry. You are building confidence and polishing technique. When the play is about to end, bust your ass up that aisle again (or take the side exit), as quickly as you both can travel without looking as if someone yelled "Fire!" Stand about twenty feet from the exit doors, pretending the chauffeur is late in picking you up. If your luck is still poor, shrug and head for the closest "nice" cocktail lounge. Do not give up the hunt. Men, I'm told, enjoy the "chase" as much as the "kill." Women, on the other hand, enjoy "trapping" their prey. Regardless, give it your best shot. Being alone at the play isn't so bad. But alone at the lounge makes it a bit too obvious. Perhaps leave your girlfriend at home during the play, but bring her along for the late evening search.

I recommend you *never* go out in a group if you want to meet a man. Wolves hunt in a pack. If you're gutsy, go out alone. The smart (and safer) approach is to go out with a girlfriend, preferably one who is less attractive than you. Of course, she might be on to your plan.

If you must travel in a pack, make advance plans in the event you choose to be "cut" from the herd should the situation warrant. Guys do it, so why not the gals too?

Ladies, here's a list of places to go to meet men! And men, now that I've done this advertising for you, *be* at these places. The stampede is about to begin.

1. BALLGAMES: This is number-one on the list because there are so many "ball" events, like baseball, football, bas-

ketball, racquetball, soccer, tennis, golf, etc. I recommend that women go to any kind of spectator game men attend. Arrive early and position yourself. If it's a golf match, walk along with the leader (more men there). At a baseball or basketball game, sit in a bleacher seat so you can move around a bit and maybe even get next to someone who looks available. If, after a short time, you wish to try your luck elsewhere, move! At a football game, choose the end zone; there might be extra seats from which to choose. And it isn't necessary to like these games. You might prefer watching your brother change a tire, but there are *men* at these events.

2. FIGHTS, KARATE CONTESTS: Maybe think about taking a course in self-defense and kill two birds with one stone; meet men and hope you never have to use what you learn. Men are likely to be the greater majority of participants at these macho strength and endurance contests.

3. OUTDOORS: I recommend only large fishing tournaments. There's no need to get up early or to actually go fishing. Just be there after turn-in to enjoy the party and awards festivities afterwards. There's boating or yacht races, jogging, canoe trips, bicycle jaunts, nature trail treks, or campouts. There are also scuba classes, tennis camps, and outdoor church picnics. On the jogging trail, why not pick out a healthy specimen and feign a minor injury a few steps after gathering all your energy and sprinting past? Anything could happen when that thoughtful jogger stops to attend your needs. Who knows, you might even *enjoy* these outdoor events!

4. GAMING and GAMBLING: Men enjoy gambling and games of all kinds — games of skill and chance. Backgammon that was ever-so-popular a decade ago is still played in many bars and clubs. Maybe look into a chess or scrabble club. Not all players are "eggheads." If you are in Las Vegas, Reno, Atlantic City or a casino in a foreign country, know these spots

are laden with big spenders and high rollers. The trouble is, these high-stake addicts see nothing while they're gambling. Maximize your visibility, get yourself a pocketful of nickles or quarters, and wander through the rows of slot machines. You can play the machines and meet men. Enjoy the game, discuss which machines have paid off, and suddenly you've made a potential new alliance, effortlessly.

5. AEROBICS CLASSES and HEALTH CLUBS: *Ahhh!* An excellent choice. So many people are weight, figure, and health conscious. It gives you the opportunity to stretch your muscles while "scoping out" the scantily clad bodies. Concentrate on your "form" during class while wearing your best leotard. And afterwards, breathlessly ask for help in weight training from that well-muscled man you've seen so often before. Plan to meet for juice or a frothy health drink after class.

6. SINGLES CLUBS: Yet another way to meet new people and cultivate new friends is through your local singles club. If you consult your yellow page telephone directory, depending on the size of your city, you might find from one to a few dozen such clubs in operation. These singles clubs usually begin with a few friends getting together to have a party. They might ask some friends to also invite friends so that everyone can meet new people and have a lot of fun in a somewhat controlled atmosphere (people who act badly are asked to leave and are never invited again). The charge to each new "member" is usually nominal, from an initiation fee to a door charge at the party itself. If the hosts are bright, they will do their utmost to see there is almost or as near to a 50/50 split in sexes as possible. This is not always easy to do. So, if you do attend one of these parties, please don't "write them off" because there were more gals than guys or vice versa. Attend a few, then decide.

The singles club idea is *wonderful!* The cost is usually less than a video dating service, but each in its own right accomplishes much the same results: you are exposed to people you probably would never have met and you have the opportunity to make a "love connection" with someone you can enjoy for a long, long time.

7. BEACHES and RESORTS: Of all the places to look for and meet the opposite sex, my favorite "hunting grounds" are beaches and resorts. First, people tend to "let it all hang loose" while on vacation, and the chances of meeting someone who would be receptive to your advances are greatly improved. They are "out of town" and out of sight of anyone who might "tell" on them. Next, they have come for "a good time," and that could mean anything from wanting to meet someone new to share their future, to wanting to just have a good time before settling back to the hum-drum life at home.

I was on vacation one time in Fort Lauderdale, Florida. Many think the majority of people there are very young. They may be right, but there were some "older" singles there too. My neck and shoulders were sore from looking in so many directions at the same time.

My very first evening in Fort Lauderdale, I was on my way to an early dinner when, in the lobby of the hotel, I spotted a girl sitting in the reception area sobbing. Oh, she was pretending to be reading a magazine, but I could see that she was in some sort of distress. I was alone and thought I might see if I could help.

Again, it takes a certain amount of boldness to take advantage of some situations. But remember: "If you don't *take* a chance, you don't *have* a chance." I sat on the rim of a large flowerpot, just a few feet to the right of the girl. Her eyes raised to meet mine, and she tried to disguise the fact that she was crying. She sniffed, made a pass at her nostrils with the handkerchief she held in one hand, and blinked her eyes, apparently trying to squeeze the tears from them.

"Hello," I said in a reasonably soft voice, with what I

thought to be a caring smile on my face. "Is there something I can do to help?"

More tears sprang from her eyes and she began to bawl. Christ! What had I gotten myself into? People were staring at us, and the girl was getting noisier by the heartbeat, especially when she tried to tell me her problem between sobs and cries and nose-clearing.

I learned that her problem was her boyfriend. He had asked her to spend a fun weekend with him at a hotel and she got upset because he signed the register "Mr. and Mrs. *Smith*." She asked him to take her home, they had an argument, and he left in a rage. Entire weekend spoiled, right? WRONG! I, Sir Galahad, a knight in slightly tarnished armor, was there to rescue her.

She freshened up in my room and accepted my dinner invitation. I vowed I would be her friend and that was the extent of it. She needed a friend and not some horny opportunist to try and "jump her bones."

We decided on having dinner at a rather "uptown" Italian restaurant. I had listened to about an hour of how great her boyfriend was and how much she loved him when I spotted two of the loveliest ladies I had seen in weeks. They were fashionably dressed, their faces were suntanned and delightful, and they were dining *alone*. Where was Brad? How could I dust off this pain-in-the-neck new "friend" without hurting her? No, I said I'd be her friend; she needed someone to help. I offered, so I would just live with it. I was half-listening to the story about more of the wonderful attributes of her angered boyfriend and how the two of them planned to get married in a few months and about the kids they would have. She wanted all boys to look *just* like their father. Whew! Single people *do* have to endure things like this once in a while.

My dinner companion excused herself to go to the bathroom. Where *was* Brad? I turned to face the girls, seated at a table just behind me. Smiling, I said, "Pardon me, I just wanted to tell each of you that you are both so terrific-looking it makes me sorry my friend Brad isn't here with me. I met this girl only an hour or so ago, crying in the lobby of my hotel. She and her boyfriend had a terrible argument . . ." I rushed through the story, trying to explain that I wasn't a jerk "scouting" while my date was in the powder room. "Yes," I repeated myself, showing a most woeful look, "Brad is a fun guy and I know you'd like him." I directed my attention to both girls, not singling a particular one out as my preference.

The girls were flattered, I could tell by their smiles. Why not? I didn't say anything wrong; in fact, they were the *right* things. Then, the one I would have chosen, a blue-eyed, tall, lean blonde with pearl-colored fingernails and a diamond studded Rolex, replied, "If Brad is *anything* like you, we too wish he were here." She looked at her girlfriend, who nodded in agreement. "In fact," she continued while reaching into her purse, "here is my telephone number (she tore the end from a check stub) and the next time you're not 'baby-sitting' please call."

My date was returning from the ladies room. I turned to face my cocktail, rose as she approached the table to help with her chair, and managed a nice smile at my *new* friends. The conclusion of this story is that it ended as quickly as it had begun. After dinner I drove directly back to the hotel and let my friend out at the entrance while I drove my car to the undercover parking. When I came into the lobby, she was wrapped in the arms of some gorilla I'm happy to say didn't see *me* coming in with her. I'm certain all was forgiven.

Hurriedly, almost in a panic, I fished the torn check stub from my jacket pocket and saw the address was in *Los Angeles!* Perhaps I'll be in that part of California one day and I'll call.

8. CHURCH GROUPS: What an *excellent* place to meet nice people. There's no guarantee, but it's the same as a college education: "doesn't mean you'll be successful but gives you more chips when you come up to the table to roll the dice."

I like church groups. And it doesn't matter what your religious preference, chances are there are many people there whom you might enjoy. Go, for instance, to the First Presbyterian, First Baptist, First Lutheran church. If, after a few weeks of visiting, you don't see anyone who catches your fancy, go to the Second Presbyterian, the Second Methodist or the Third, and so on. *Increase your chances!* Get the odds in your favor. You don't even have to go to church — just the group after church. If you are a nice person and just don't know where to go to meet people, staying at home on Sunday morning is not the answer. Church is!

THE POSSIBILITIES ARE EVERYWHERE

There are *so* many places to meet the opposite sex. There are car washes, grocery stores, banks, shopping malls, bookstores, outdoor art exhibits, fairs, parades, grand openings, mixers, or cook-offs. Any function where a crowd attends will have men and women. Try them all and have fun doing it. You're staying busy and have less time to think about the one who just walked out. Yes, turn the page on that chapter the same as you're doing with this one, and look for something (and someone) new! Make a list of the functions you would like to attend . . . and *attend* them!

These are my hobbies and interests:

1.

2.

3.

4.

5.

Where to Find a New Companion

6.

7.

8.

Some of the functions I could enjoy alone or with a friend:

1.

2.

3.

4.

5.

6.

Calendar:

Party/Event: _____
Place/Date/Time: _____
New Acquaintances/Phone Numbers: _____

Party/Event: _____
Place/Date/Time: _____
New Acquaintances/Phone Numbers: _____

Party/Event: _____
Place/Date/Time: _____
New Acquaintances/Phone Numbers: _____

Party/Event: _____
Place/Date/Time: _____
New Acquaintances/Phone Numbers: _____

Party/Event: _____
Place/Date/Time: _____
New Acquaintances/Phone Numbers: _____

Party/Event: _____
Place/Date/Time: _____
New Acquaintances/Phone Numbers: _____

Party/Event: _____
Place/Date/Time: _____
New Acquaintances/Phone Numbers: _____

Party/Event: _____
Place/Date/Time: _____
New Acquaintances/Phone Numbers: _____

Party/Event: _____
Place/Date/Time: _____
New Acquaintances/Phone Numbers: _____

Where to Find a New Companion

Chapter Eleven

How to Approach Someone

There are countless ways to get someone's attention without making a complete jackass of yourself. In an earlier chapter, I suggested the old ploy of "dropping your handkerchief" or maybe even "bumping someone with a drink in their hands." What happens when one of these corn ploys works? What do you say in order to interest this person once you get their attention? Here are some examples.

One of the absolute corniest approaches I've ever seen used was when I was in the service. Three of us, all slicked down in our freshly pressed uniforms with our sharpshooter badges worn proudly over our left shirt pocket, were walking around the business area of a small southern town. Girls were circling in cars, waving and laughing. Then an innovative buddy of mine spotted this parked car and walked toward it. He stuffed his hat into his back pocket, unbuttoned his top shirt button, loosened his tie, and walked out from behind the car and waved for assistance. Wouldn't you know it, the very first car to stop was filled with half a dozen girls! While being bright enough to get them to stop and notice, he still struck out. He was so darned pleased with his keen idea, he simply "dropped the ball." After he had smiled at the girls and admitted it was not his car and he had just wanted them to stop, the girls giggled and drove off.

This chapter discusses how *not* to drop the ball when a situation presents itself. First of all, it takes a certain amount of bravado to introduce yourself to a complete stranger. One way to conquer nervousness is to think about all those evenings alone. The other way is to be fortified with some good approach lines, ones that will work.

Every day, walking down the street, you pass people you'd like to meet. If they aren't stopped by being initiated into a conversation, they'll keep passing you by, right? Why not try a direct approach like: "Excuse me, but if I let you walk by without saying hello or trying to get you to join me for a cup of coffee, I'll just hate myself." This, believe it or not, works! Oh, sure, some will be married, some will smile back and keep walking, but no one has been offended and you just might strike paydirt. It doesn't matter whether you're male or female. It's probably easier for a man to do it, but why not a woman? I would be enthralled if some attractive girl stopped me, and chances are the women would certainly be flattered if you asked them. Nothing ventured, nothing gained.

Suppose you're in a grocery store and see an attractive man looking at the gourmet food shelf. It's easy to go up and ask a question like "Do you prefer this sauce or that?" This is a sure way of striking up a conversation. The same holds true for a liquor store. First, learn a bit about wines. If you see someone looking over a bottle of wine you happen to be familiar with, why not walk up and say, "I see you looking at this bottle of '78 Valpolichella. I've found the '70 to be less expensive and a bit drier. It tastes wonderful with my famous lasagna." Perhaps act a bit embarrassed, maybe drop your eyelids and pretend to be shy (if you're a girl). And if you're a guy,

How to Approach Someone

why not puff up a bit when bragging on your cooking skills? It could be a nice beginning. Just hope they don't know a lot about wine or you will be "caught." But then, so what? You can both laugh about it while having lasagna at your apartment.

My buddy Brad, whom I mention so often, is an expert at making conversation over anything. First of all, he knows all the right things to say and doesn't hold back. He acts a bit awkward at times, but can recite Shakespeare and tell you about every composer, every waltz, every broadway play down to the hit tunes over the past thirty years, and even punk rock. He knows it all! His finds include girls in the grocery store, the dentist's office, the record shop, and even at the car wash. He just smiles, puts on a friendly look and walks right up to her, then talks about how beautiful her teeth are. Sometimes he squeezes fruit for her, or gets one of those see-through cellophane bags for her grapes while discussing the new car wash that squirts a so-called "love scent" in the car. Yep, he meets them and is very successful with his approaches.

One day at the music store, Brad walked up to a girl who was looking at a complicated piece of stereo equipment and asked if he could show her how it worked.

"Are you a salesman?" the girl asked.

"If I were," Brad replied, "I'd have been over here the second you stopped. In fact," he continued with a smile, "I'd have followed you around the store."

Nice line, huh? Not offensive, complimentary in fact, and to the point. If there was any interest, Brad would make a new friend. A girl can do pretty much the same thing, you know. Just walk up and assist someone you feel might be interesting. Spend a few moments to help. Even if it doesn't work out to your satisfaction, you at least tried and will feel good about helping others.

Let's suppose you're at a party and it begins to drag a little. The hostess wasn't aware enough to try and match you with someone, or maybe you have just separated, divorced, or broken up. The hostess (or host) was friends with each of you and doesn't want to go out on a limb to make a match for fear of hurting your "ex." Now is the time to, again, make the first step. Just walk up to the first person you are attracted to and say, "Let's show these people how to have fun. C'mon, let's dance." Another good party line is "So-and-so invited me over to meet one of her friends. I'm hoping it was you!" Again, a mildly brazen line, but bright and to the point.

When at a club, the best way to meet someone is to dance. You get to hold them without getting clobbered, can chat one-on-one without others breaking in, and have given yourself a chance to not be lonely. If, after that first dance, you like them, ask for another dance and take it from there.

You're driving along the highway and spot some attractive people at a flea market. Those markets are all over the place and are always interesting. Stop and manuever your way around until you spot the "prey" looking over an item. Then say something cute like, "I see we have the same interest in (whatever he or she is holding up)." Yes, no matter what, make conversation. Make an effort, and be a bit innovative while doing so.

While in the drug store, you notice someone looking over a vast array of vitamins. Everybody, it seems, is taking vitamins today. I am, aren't you? It's easy to meet someone at the vitamin counter. Simply mention some new vitamins on the market and what they do. In minutes that person will be telling about *their* vitamins and what works for them. "Say, would you like to have some herbal tea or juice, and continue our discussion?" Simple, eh? Of course it is, and you don't even have to be *brave* to do it. Just be sincere, with an ulterior motive. Naturally, it was contrived, but who cares? You might be doing everyone a favor, so don't pass up the opportunity. Just use an approach, no matter how corny. It'll work.

I had another buddy named Ray. What a hunter! He'd

walk through the downtown offices of the company reputed to have the best-looking girls, and he'd just visit, dressed in his finest. Once spotting a secretary who suited his taste, he'd give her his card, make light conversation, and ask her name. Then he'd shoot downstairs to the flower shop and have one rose delivered to the girl with his card attached. You'd be surprised how many called him back that evening to thank him for the thoughtful little gift. If there was no return call, he'd visit again in a few days and ask the girl to lunch. There was tremendous success with this approach, but then, Ray was a professional. He might have been lonely more often than we suspect, but he was rarely alone!

Another way to meet the opposite sex is to appear helpless. A girlfriend has left and you are now faced with the chore of doing laundry. So what? Make the best of it. If living in an apartment complex, use the laundry room there, but wait until someone cute walks in to do her clothes. Hustle in with a pile of dirty togs. Ask for help. "Do I put the soap in here, or here?" Or, "Do you have some extra quarters?" Anything, say *anything* to break the ice and start a conversation. "I live in 187," you might add. "And I barbecue chicken unlike the world has ever known. Would you like to join me the next time I cook out?" Either sex can use these lines.

A better place might be the community laundromat. There could be a dozen "possibles" in there of both sexes. Recently divorced or separated men and women are all eager to meet someone. If the person is married, tell them your present predicament and maybe they'll invite you over to dinner or a party and introduce you to someone. Everybody has a friend they'd like to pawn off on someone new. This will give exposure in meeting new people while allowing you to make the actual selection.

If there was only limited success with the laundromat at the apartment complex, why not try the pool? Smile when others pass by. Say "Hello" or ask if they'd like a cold glass of tea, or on Saturday or Sunday mornings, have a pitcher of Bloody Marys handy and a few extra styrofoam cups. Surely someone who is attractive will be nursing a hangover. It's easy to look to the side and say, "I have the most delicious Bloody Marys in the area. Would you like to try one?" They'll either say yes or no, but you've broken the ice and opened the door to further conversation, maybe even a friendship.

There's probably a girl at the office who has caught your eye many times and you're not certain what approach to take. Just try the direct approach. Ask her to coffee or to lunch. One book told about how a fellow started a conversation with a girl who was always busily working around the office. She'd be typing, running in and out of the office, getting coffee. He could never get her to stay in one place long enough to say more than a hello.

He tried a direct approach, but with a bit of finesse. When walking into the office one morning, Miss Always Busy was on one of her flights out of the office. He reached out, gently grasped her arm, and said, "Dating you would be like dating a harem."

Miss Busy looked over and just *had* to ask, "Why?" Unoffensive, a bit bold, certainly startling to the busy secretary, but it prompted an immediate response.

"Because, you seem to do the job of half a dozen people and I haven't been able to get you to slow down long enough to ask you out for this evening."

She was flattered by the fact someone noticed how industrious she was. He caused her to drop her guard. She smiled, tossed her head to the side, took off her glasses, and then he shifted into second gear. In complete amazement he continued, "I think you're beautiful with or without those glasses. Meet you at the cooler after work and you pick the place, OK?" It worked!

How about those times at the shopping mall when you've spotted an attractive girl trying on a dress or a hat? If they seem pleased with the article while consulting the mirror, give a compliment. If they seem undecided, offer an opinion. The salesperson will normally step aside and appreciate any help offered. Once having commented on the dress or hat, ask if you can see a few more things she has chosen. She'll *love* it! Why hadn't her boyfriend or ex-husband been this interested in what she purchased? If they had, she wouldn't be available for such attention. But she is, and you gave it to her. Be honest in the appraisal of what she is trying on. Be sincere with your help, and you just might strike up a match.

WHAT TO DO AFTER "HELLO"

Let's say you go into a bar and there, sitting alone, is a person you'd like to meet. This is probably easier for a guy, but it could be a good approach for a bold woman also. Manage to seat yourself right next to this person who, apparently, is alone. Just make a turn in their direction, place a hand lightly on theirs, and wear a nice smile. They'll look over to you and hopefully won't jump out of their seat. If they do, you were too abrupt. Spend a moment or two before trying this, making sure that they are settled, not deep in thought, and are aware someone is next to them. Again, a warm, sincere, caring smile is essential with this tactic. "Let me buy you a double and maybe that would help whatever is troubling you." She will surely make some reply, maybe only "thank you," but then you can say whatever comes to mind. Or, she could say "no thank you," giving a hint to go into plan B. "Sorry if I offended you. It's just that you looked as if you needed a friend. I've felt the way you appear to be feeling when something unexpected, negative, or hurtful happened to me. I hope it works out for you." Then turn away and mind your own business. If you haven't offended them, chances are they will apologize, continue to ignore you, or accept your kindness. What have you lost? Nothing ventured, nothing gained. You were only being nice.

After getting the other person's attention, don't sit there like a dolt or you'll miss out. This is why it helps to have several *interests* to share. Continue to lavish attention and be helpful and considerate of the other person. Be fun and interesting. No matter where you find someone to your liking, take control of the situation after getting them into your web with a cutesy little line.

Go places they want to go and discover how often they reciprocate. Try some different restaurants, unusual clubs, or adventurous activities. The more involved, the better chance you have of never being dull, bored, *or* lonely.

A guy can open a door for a woman, ask if she needs help with her groceries or packages. Be assertive — reach out to help with the bundles. "Here, let me help you with these." When reaching for the packages, this prompts an ordinary response to hand over a partial load. Then introduce yourself and you're on your way!

These approaches can be used anywhere: at the airport, hospital, in a cafeteria line, at the magazine counter, grocery store, liquor store, cleaners, in an office, at the pool, anywhere!

Even try them at church, or rather after church, when there's coffee and cookies at the fellowship meeting. Brad and I once attended an afternoon church function. The nice assistant minister asked everyone to stand and introduce themselves, then relate the reason for their presence. I stood up and said I had come to "be in the midst of nice people," which sounded like a good approach. Brad got up and said, "I'm here because I wanted to meet girls." The group laughed and then applauded Brad's honesty. Many, I'm certain, were there for the same reason, but tried to disguise it with little niceties. Brad, on the other hand, came directly to the point. After the social, we met many eligible girls and again laughed about it. I strung along with Brad and took advantage of his honest and direct approach to share some of the booty. Funny *and* fun, eh?

START TRAINING NOW

Practice the various techniques mentioned in this chapter. Stand before a mirror and maybe even get a tape recorder to see how you look and sound. Those not at ease with the first several attempts can make changes, but at least try something. The more prepared, the better trained, and the more confident you are, the better your chances are for success. There are far too many lonely people out there looking for someone else. Be one of the few who know how to begin a conversation and "keep the ball rolling." Many of these approaches were for the men, but some can be shared. Why not give the guy at the office a call and ask him over for dinner? It's easy to do with some guts — and a plan. Tell him he seems nice and maybe if he doesn't have any plans, how about meeting at the pizza joint? Or maybe he would prefer to come over and share the dinner you have prepared.

Invite him to go sailing for the coming weekend or say you have an extra ticket to a play, the circus, or whatever special event is in town. Why not try? Don't hesitate and wait too long, or some other imaginative person in that office may speak up first. Of course, there are always the old high school tricks. Remember how well they worked? Get a girlfriend to slip him the word you are interested. It's kid stuff, I know, but effective. Then, the next time he says hello, follow through with that dinner invitation.

I interviewed over 500 women and asked them a variety of questions on what they did when they asked a guy out and what was the outcome of that date. Their ages ran from twenty to fifty. Some were quite shy and it was difficult prying information out of them. These were the ones who not only attested to being alone, but sometimes avoided potential suitors.

One petite interviewee told me how sad and lonely she was, but admitted also that she was afraid to make a fool of herself. A few bad experiences with men who had tried to manipulate her into the sack on the first date made her resign to just let the world pass her by. She was alone. She neither had a roommate nor a pet, but did have a friend across town stuck in the same type of situation.

Still others were not afraid to ask men for a date. "When I saw Gilbert at the meat counter of the supermarket and noticed he wasn't wearing a wedding band, I introduced myself and asked if he'd like the pork chops he was inspecting prepared in my special way. He nodded yes, and we have been together ever since, eleven years," stated Cynthia, a schoolteacher, who gets a round of applause.

"I was afraid to ask a man out on a date," said Gladys, a twenty-six-year-old secretary. "I always let them do the asking. Then, a girlfriend and I were discussing men and realized 'equality' also meant our right to choose. The next day, when that new salesman came to the office, I asked him if he'd like to go on a picnic. He accepted and we dated for a few months. I may be a little slow to catch on, but I like the idea of being liberated."

Why not, ladies, approach a man? This world has changed. Those who allow what looks like an opportunity to pass by just have to wait. Who knows how long it'll be until the next time? Men enjoy being sought after by interesting women. Just be at ease when introducing yourself and beginning a conversation. He will respond favorably if interested. And if not, don't worry — he won't embarrass you. So what is there to lose? Give it a try. Men have been doing it for years. Now it's your turn.

At a seminar in Chicago for several hundred women, one blurted out: "I simply refuse to play the game." My answer: "It's all a game, lady. If you don't play the game, chances are you'll never be *in* the game."

Chapter Twelve

Video Dating

There are those who scoff at the idea of video dating, but please, read about it first and then decide. Skeptics will say they "prefer getting their own dates," but when just arriving in a new town, having recently been divorced or "ending it" with a companion, you are alone and lonely and need all the help available. Some will say: "Who wants a blind date that you pay for?" It isn't like that at all! Others will say it's like being on an "auction block," or call it a "Lonely Hearts Club" and dozens of other tasteless, nonthinking comments. They are all entitled to their opinion, but you — who are lonely — give it a try! It can be *wonderful!*

This is how it works. There might be an ad in the paper or on television. Copy the phone number and make the call. Office hours vary, but most video dating services make it convenient to call. In many instances they stay open as late as nine in the evening, and certainly the same on weekends. Most refrain from quoting prices on the telephone, but the service is affordable to almost everyone. Make an appointment and go to their office for an interview or just "to look things over." There is rarely any pressure. A charming receptionist will greet you at the door and give you a tour, while explaining the benefits. One room will have stacks of albums — some with information on men, and others on women. Look at either or both sets of books to give you an idea not only of what you might expect to find in a date, but also about your competition.

It's great fun just visiting. The albums are listed alphabetically. For example, the female "C" book will have names like Carole, Catherine, Claudette (first names only). There is at least one photograph of each person in the album. A recent photo is requested. The agency will provide a Polaroid if you don't have one available. Next to the photo is an information sheet giving the name, age, height, weight, hair color, eye color, marital status, number of children and their ages, drinking or smoking and religious preference, political affiliation, and a few other tidbits of information. There is also a space provided for you to fill in an age-range preference for those who will request you as a potential date. The other side of the page has more questions like:

1. Describe yourself as you feel your best friend would.

2. List three of your best attributes.

3. What would you like to do on a date?

4. What kind of person would you like to date?

5. Tell something about yourself you'd like others to know.

Many go through volume after volume looking at photos, checking vital statistics, then settling on two or three choices; some choose a dozen. Each photo has a number. Carole, for instance, might be 211, Veronica is 94, and Janine is 14. Then go to the videotape library and select the tapes matching these numbers. Take these tapes to a private booth equipped with a television and VCR. While watching a ten-minute cassette and listening through earphones, you can study your "prospect" while he or she is answering questions, such as:

1. How long have you lived in this area?
2. Where is your original home?
3. What sports do you like? Like to dance? Sing? Ride horses? Go out to dinner? Beat your dog? Go to church?

The interviewer asks questions and allows the subject time to tell some cute or nice or naughty things about themselves. The tape should give a pretty good idea what to expect.

After looking at several tapes, you may then select the person(s) you'd like to date. Give their name(s) and number(s) to the counselor, who will put these numbers in a file and mark your number on the card(s) selected. Then, each person selected is called or sent a postcard stating they have been picked by three or four (or however many) people. The subject comes into the office/studio, looks at your photo, checks *your* vital statistics, and reads about your likes and dislikes. If interested, they will match your number to the videotape and watch *your* interview. If they like you, they will also report to the counselor, who will then notify you that numbers 89, 106, and 22 have responded positively to your inquiries. Full names and telephone numbers are provided, enabling you to call at your convenience. If you change your mind, or the situation has changed, it isn't necessary to call. There is no obligation.

After you select the date you'd like to have (or feel you would) and they've selected you, go about this in an academic fashion. Do *not* waste an evening with a nerd (or a nerdette). Agree to meet at some public place for a cocktail or cup of coffee for fifteen or so minutes. After that brief visit, you'll know whether you want to spend an evening with that person. Be *smart* about dating.

A METHOD THAT WORKS

There are several advantages to video dating. You get to look at hundreds of photos and read many things about people who seem compatible to you. You see a recent tape (waist up) and can tell whether their looks and vital statistics suit you. Also, it's possible to become familiar with the person chosen before actually having to meet them. Females usually feel more secure knowing everyone participating in the service has been checked out. Potentially "strange" individuals are denied memberships. Too, if you feel uncomfortable or that your date is too unusual, incidents can be reported to the counselor. The chances of the date being "successful" are multiplied over a casual bar pick-up or fix-up with someone's cousin, because the two of you are guaranteed to have much in common.

I made three different tapes, solely for the purpose of research, you understand. In one tape I played the part of the rich playboy, telling of my Mercedes, my yacht, and requesting girls no closer to my age than fifteen years. In the second tape my purpose was to appear more settled, even stodgy. For the third tape, I tried to be Mr. Perfect, ranting on about wanting but one woman to spoil and share in my life. I vowed to love and be faithful only to her, take her to foreign countries, big dinner parties, the opera and the ballet. I mentioned that gourmet cooking was one hobby and I loved to prepare exquisite dinners. Occupation was listed as an "author," and I spoke of making a promise to myself to "go only first class" in everything. My interests included a love of children (in reality, I'd prefer to have sixty ducks in my bedroom rather than one baby) and stated that if the other person had any children, I yearned to be a perfect daddy to them. Was that strong? My card on that tape was filled in three days with over fifty inquiries.

The playboy tape also brought in some interesting requests. My choice was a twenty-three-year-old hairdresser who looked absolutely *wild* with long, black hair seeming to be in constant disarray. Her green cat-eyes and photo in a swimsuit were all that were necessary to turn my head. The icing on that gorgeous cake told me that she liked exciting places, weekend trips, that she didn't drink much but would certainly get drunk with the right person; that she wanted to do anything to please. Her name was Crissy.

We met in a noisy lounge, shook hands, sat at the bar, and yelled niceties at each other, neither hearing half of what the other said. She liked me, I could tell, and I liked her. I dressed in slacks and an open-collar shirt with my new, bad-taste one-ounce gold bar hanging on a solid gold chain. She wore dress slacks and a reasonably snug-fitting sweater. It seems we each wanted to show off what we considered our main attributes. From what conversation I was able to hear, she didn't seem overly bright, but since this was research, I wasn't about to ask for her Phi Beta Kappa key. After ordering frozen strawberry daiquiris, we sipped them for several minutes and smiled at each other.

When we finished the drinks, I took her by the arm and steered her toward the door. "Let's have dinner on my boat," I announced. "Samuel has prepared some delightful hors d'oeurves and it's a nice drive to the bay. I'll have you home in a few hours if you'd like." I led her to the Mercedes and could tell she was in awe.

It pleased me, even though it was unfair, maybe even a bit cruel. But I promised that if Crissy was to be *the* one, I'd *teach* her to read and write. I was twenty and some odd years older than Crissy, but kept in good physical shape. My hair was lightly mottled with gray. That didn't shake my security, as nobody had ever cringed at the sight of me. Yep, I was in complete control. A Mercedes, a yacht, a chef preparing dinner — who wouldn't be?

The boat was a forty-six-foot, twelve-year-old Owens cruiser with enough cabin room for a dining area, living area, captain's quarters, and two smaller cabins. There was a bath with commode, shower, and vanity. It took lots of maintenance because of the wood and brass, but the *Happy Bachelor* was, nonetheless, impressive. Samuel, my part-time yardman, looked elegant in my last year's tux and could use the fifty bucks for his few hours of effort for the evening. He added just the right touch.

The hors d'oeuvres were cold boiled shrimp, oysters, some awful-tasting caviar from the gourmet section of the supermarket, and a large salad. The cold champagne was the *pièce de résistance*. I began to feel like the playboy described in my tape. Samuel excused himself within half an hour. The moon was out and the weather was perfect. I put on some smooth FM tape and we slow-danced on the stern, an area about six by eight feet. We didn't require much room.

Crissy was really impressed. She said so numerous times. When the song paused I kissed her three or four times with kisses not exceedingly long nor wet. I know I could have charmed her into the captain's cabin, but I truly liked her. She was sweet, warm, and extraordinarily beautiful. Deciding to be truthful with her, I told her about doing research for an upcoming novel. She said she respected me for my honesty, but added that it didn't matter. She was having a wonderful time. I still felt guilty.

I drove Crissy back to the club and followed her in my car to her apartment. She waved me to come inside. We talked, held hands, kissed a few more times, and I ended up keeping her company for the remainder of the night. We saw each other several times after that night, then I introduced her to the son of a friend. Several months have passed and they are still "going steady." Lucky guy!

My second date was with someone who chose *me*. I looked over her photo, file and tape, then decided it was time to do some research. She selected the tape that was "Mr. Perfect." One of the statements made was that I wanted someone to be faithful to me, someone I could trust. She reasoned, apparently through amateur psychology, that I had been hurt in love as she had, and thought we could spend some time crying on each other's shoulders. She wanted a husband badly and immediately! Her name was Marcia. She was a few years older than I, was quite attractive, and seemed bright, judging from her taped interview, plus she was rich. Opera and ballet were two interests we held in common.

Marcia was going to turn the "Crissy" routine on me! I drove to the most exclusive part of town and parked my car in front of a castle-like mansion. A limousine and a Mercedes sportscar sat in the circular drive. A butler answered the bell and ushered me into the Dunhill Room. While I was waiting for my date, one of the three maids in sight served me a martini. Within five minutes Marcia came floating down the huge staircase "a la Loretta Young," all smiles and heavily bejeweled. At her suggestion, we had the chauffeur drive us to her club. She had the evening well planned. I felt like I was in a trap. *Touché!* Repayment for my efforts with Crissy.

Since it was Marcia's evening, I allowed her to order for me: Chateaubriand for two, Dom Perignon, candlelight, and a talented pianist playing soft, sweet songs of the fifties. I finished my plate, but Marcia only took two small bites. She was spending her time sitting upright in the chair, head moving right and left like a weathervane in changing winds, hands waving at whomever was in sight. Yes, it was Marcia's night to show off. She was proud of me. I was flattered. When friends and acquaintances stopped at our table, she was quick to introduce me as an author, telling all they must surely have heard of me. I'll bet all of those super-rich, nice folks would have fainted if they had known Marcia got me through a video dating service. Still, she was proud and I felt complimented. Marcia was a nice person who did lots of charity work, was a devout Christian and a pillar of society. She was a striking woman who wielded her power and position with poise and dignity. The evening was a delight. It was an experience I enjoyed.

Back at her home, after our coffee liqueur and fifteen-minute chat in the Dunhill Room, I put out my hand to say goodnight. She came toward me and made an attempt at kissing me, but the kiss fell short and there were only sounds of lips smacking. I did the same, so, what the heck! I never called her again, but do see her name in the "columns" having returned from here or there, or doing her charity work. She's one helluva catch for someone. There are many Marcias enrolled with video services.

I had several more dates, but most were similar. Not to shortchange the women, I enlisted the help of a girlfriend of mine to choose some male dates. Here's her report.

Let's call her Jane, who is in her mid-twenties, a secretary for an oil executive, and divorced. The first date she had was with Willard. Willard was in his early forties, divorced, lived in a big house and had his picture taken standing next to his Rolls. Willard met Jane at his club. She drove her Toyota past the large iron gates and felt she had made a wrong turn. The most inexpensive car in the lot was a Cadillac. The valet parked her little yellow car and gave Jane directions to the Walnut Room, where Willard was stationed at the bar, dressed in a three-piece gray suit. His hair was neatly blow-dried and combed, he smelled of expensive aftershave, and he had a smile as wide as a Warsaw Grouper.

Willard escorted Jane to a table by the window overlooking the golf course and lake. They had cocktails. Four doubles later, Willard began a spiel about how he'd like to be a male duck. They don't work, live at the country club without paying dues, get the best food in leftovers, and can "grab any female duck by the head with their bill and do as they please." Jane reacted with a shocked giggle, somewhere between laughing *at* Willard and feeling sorry for him. Willard didn't order food and proceeded to get drunker. Jane excused herself for a trip to the powder room, rushed for her car, and drove home. The next day she told the service about Willard and he was called in for a review. Within three days, Willard's photo and tape had been removed.

Another date Jane accepted was with an attorney. Let's call him Tom. Tom had been married thrice, had three kids, divorced seven years, and was a charmer. He had it all. He was tall, very good-looking, and had a good practice (handled only large divorce cases). Tom, who picked Jane up at her apartment, was dressed in slacks and a sports shirt. He took her to a strange little Italian restaurant, talked of world events, and asked about Jane. He downplayed his attributes, but slyly let things "slip out" here and there, inviting a question from Jane which he promptly and humbly would answer. He was an attorney, all right.

They went to a new disco to dance, and ended the evening with one sweet, short goodnight kiss at the door. He turned and walked to his car, neglecting to mention whether he would like to see her again. Jane wondered what she had done wrong. He seemed like such a nice guy and she thought he liked her. Jane couldn't recall saying anything that would have upset him. "Hmmm, strange," she mused. But that sly fox Tom had a *plan*. After fifteen minutes or so passed, he called her from his car telephone. "Hello, Jane? This is Tom. What I meant to ask is — see me tomorrow evening, won't you? I had a terrific time and I'd like to know you better." Jane was in ecstasy. Tom's plan worked. Jane knew it was contrived, but she still went for it. Smooth, huh? Those two are still seeing each other regularly.

This method of meeting people is a truly superior one. I cannot see one flaw in the entire plan and would recommend it to my mother, daughter, friend, or ex-wife. If it offends you to make use of one of these services, you are wrong! It is more offensive to me and more oppressive to you to remain lonely. If you are new in town, or are divorced, widowed, or recovering from a lost love, video dating is a very successful way to find someone. Think about it. I give video dating the highest rating. It's fun! Try it!

Chapter Thirteen

Let's Keep 'Em Once We Get 'Em

You have made a list of prerequisites, have pages of things you refuse to accept, and have found that someone special in your life. Now, what will add to the chances of having this person *remain* in your company? How to show him or her happiness and enjoyment? What can be done so the two of you can share the times spent together in mutual fulfillment? Maybe it isn't even someone new, but you feel your old relationship is lessening in desire and adventure, and you want to keep that relationship intact.

The three "Cs" are the answer: *communication, consideration,* and *compromise.* Yes, let's keep 'em once we get 'em.

In the preceding chapters we've talked about things to do to get someone new, plus things *not* to do once a romance has ended. We had a chapter on how to cope with divorce and separation, then a few dozen places to find someone new. Now, let's get right at *keeping* this person you love.

First of all, it is a two-way street. A romance cannot last when one person does all the compromising, when one person has all the consideration, and when two people cannot communicate. Let's begin with *communication.*

One man interviewed was ten days from his divorce being final. His wife of eight years was living with her parents, sixty miles away. They had three young children. From the five or so hours spent with this young man, I determined he had many good points. He was bright, polite, and loved his wife and children. He was a good-looking guy, kept in shape with tennis and swimming, and seemed to have a pleasant personality. The fellow stated he always helped his wife with the household chores, like washing dishes, doing laundry, and even cooking. She worked a full-time job, and he was happy to share the chores at home.

His wife, though, did not like the fact she had to work. She griped about it often, but there wasn't anything he could do about it. His business kept them in necessities, but *her* income surely came in handy for the comforts. From what I was hearing, surely they had a lack of communication.

Her parents also had a habit of interfering. They felt their daughter "should have married a man who could support his family." Several times a month the couple were invited over for dinner with her parents. The young man was never comfortable visiting, since he knew how they felt about him. Why in the *world* didn't he tell his wife about it? He admitted it would upset his wife if they didn't see her family, and he didn't want to do that. So, the result was a pending divorce.

Upon my instructions, he made a list of good things about his wife and a list of things he would like to change. They were to have dinner in a few days to discuss the children, and I advised him to ask her to make a similar list. If they exchanged those "like" and "gripe" lists, it would be the beginning of communication between two folks so desperately searching for the right answers.

From her list, he found she didn't mind working, but not a full-time job. She also enjoyed her duties in the kitchen and other household chores; it made her feel more like a woman and closer to the children. His list told about her bad moods and how he disliked having dinner with her parents, since they disapproved of him.

The solution was so profoundly simple it's frightening. She got a *part-time* job. That way she could attend to the so-called "wifely" chores while he relaxed or played with the kids. They learned to be more conservative on money spent for recreation, like going on picnics and taking the kids to the beach to build sand castles and play in the surf. Instead of ordering fast food for dinner, because they were both so tired after a long day, the wife was able to cook more at home. And once she stopped griping about full-time employment, the parents got "off hubby's back" and dinners together became fun. Her moodiness disappeared. Within three short months, they were a happy and loving family.

This method is not a new one. It was used a few decades back when companies brought their employees into a group and had them write things they thought about each other. Make a list of the things you like about this person and (hopefully) a shorter list of what the problem areas are.

I *implore* those of you who are married with children to play together and pray together. Go fishing or watch softball games with "him and the boys" and you, go to the piano recital or ballgames with "her and the girls." Too often people who are married with children neglect each other and stop doing things as a family. One day, the kids are grown up and gone and you are sitting across the table from a stranger. If you *are* a family, *function* as a family.

The above story has a happy ending, but several others do not. Another couple also suffered from a communication problem. In this case, the husband was a complete idiot who insisted on having his night out with the boys so he could have the time to "fool around" a little on the side. Of course he would never allow his *wife* the same privileges. After completing their lists, it was painful to read what he expected to achieve in order to be happy. If his wife had read this book and made her lists prior to their marriage, there would not have been a marriage. She would have gotten rid of him after the first date.

The last two couples discovered their differences to be too numerous to alter and decided to proceed with the divorce and seek companionship elsewhere. It is hoped that they will each employ their newfound knowledge before embarking on a new, serious relationship.

I'd like married couples to remain married — happily. If you've tried all available means of doing so (talking to friends, clergy, psychiatrists, counselors, each other) and there is no solution, I recommend a dissolution of the marriage. I'm telling you not from a religious or moral viewpoint but from a practical one.

GET THE WORD OUT: COMMUNICATE

Yes, communication is important. Find the time to talk things over with your companion. If something is a problem, why not bring it out in the open, get it off your chest, and solve it? Sometimes it is something so simple, so trivial, that the two of you will laugh and find a solution in a matter of minutes.

If you can't find the right words during a discussion, remember to write them down. One friend, whom I dearly love, is selfish. He is so preoccupied with his own problems he just doesn't concern himself with the problems or efforts of others. After hearing him make a stupid comment, rather than start an argument by correcting him, I simply go home, think about it, and write him a letter on my feelings. When he gets the letter, there is time to absorb the words and thoughts, and then he calls me and we discuss it. In fact, now, when he feels I am wrong, he writes to *me*.

Communication is essential in a relationship between

friends, lovers, and others. The entire world revolves around communication. Everyone from heads-of-state to criminals need communication. It is the only method of conveying a message, of "selling" a product or idea, or making others understand how we feel.

BE CONSIDERATE

The second big "C" in a relationship is *consideration*. Wow! What a fine word. It is probably *the* most important word in the entire world. Dictionaries have varying definitions, depending on how the word is used. The only definition I care to pursue is "thoughtfulness of others."

A considerate person will not be late for an appointment, because they are considerate of the other person's time.

To be considerate means not saying unkind words about others because it might cause them unhappiness.

If you are considerate, you will be truthful and faithful and helpful to others.

Yes, to call a person *considerate* is a fine compliment. Consideration of a loved one takes in a large range of feelings and actions. A considerate person would never leave a stack of dirty dishes for the hostess to clean up. Nor would he join a friend on a fishing trip, then leave the friend to clean the boat. A considerate person would not gobble up all the dessert before allowing others to sample it. The list is endless.

Being considerate simply means following the golden rule: "Do unto others as you would have them do unto you." True consideration probably goes even beyond that. Perhaps it doesn't matter if the person before you doesn't flush the toilet. Nevertheless, flush it when *you're* finished, huh? Perhaps you don't mind waiting ten or fifteen minutes on a curb for someone to pick you up, but it could be the one you are late for does mind. In this case, communication is essential so you can have consideration.

Consideration means that, if your dog has a habit of barking in the middle of the night and disturbing the neighbors, either train the dog, get rid of it, move, or wrap the dog's mouth with air conditioning duct tape. If it's discovered the neighbors within "bark-shot" are both deaf, then there is no problem. If you learn they have soundproofed their homes against inconsiderate assholes who have barking dogs, you have no problem. Simple when you think about it, isn't it? These are forms of consideration.

An example of consideration between two people who love each other could best be expressed by my tale of Mary, a woman who works in one of my businesses. She and Lee have been married for thirty-eight years. Lee worked as a millwright who had the graveyard shift — midnight until eight in the morning. They lived in a small country town about sixty miles from where Lee was employed. Mary would prepare Lee "breakfast" about ten in the evening. Afterwards, Lee would go to work (an hour and ten minute trek). He worked this shift for fifteen years. Every morning at four, when Lee had his "lunch" hour, Mary was in the parking lot waiting for him with a hot meal, *every* morning for the entire fifteen years. This was love, and care, and *consideration*.

These two lovely people cared for each other and were willing to be "considerate" of each other. Mary reasoned, "If Papa can drive in and work, the least I can do is to see he has a good hot meal in his stomach." That, my friends, is one of the sweetest stories I have encountered in many years about two people successfully in love.

LEARN TO COMPROMISE

The third of my big "Cs" is *compromise*. A few months ago, when you made your list and found a partner, he or she was nearly perfect, right? Well, perhaps your eyes were dulled by the magic of a new romance, and you overlooked some of the minor frailties of your companion. Now it's time to change them, right? *Wrong!* Remember, there are two kinds of people some of you want — the person you dream about and the person that doesn't exist. These are the only "perfect" people. Maybe if and when you become perfect you can demand the same, but eventually you'll notice your partner might possess a few habits not to your liking. Then there will have to be a compromise on a few of your own quirks that might be irritating to him or her. You might have to compromise a lot.

If she wants you to have dinner at her parents' house, why not accompany her without obvious resentment? Don't show the rope burns on your wrists where she had to drag you. Once in a while, sacrifice a few hours or a day here and there in order to make your partner happy. Then, when an old buddy comes to visit and stays a few extra days, she might not gripe so loudly. You two have compromised!

If she would like you to go shopping with her, why not try it? Not a lot of men do. It doesn't have to become a habit, you understand, but now and then (especially if it's a new outfit for a special occasion) go along and do it.

He wants you to watch him play golf? Go with him. Just ride around in the cart and marvel at his shotmaking. Do *not* bring along the Walkman and listen to taped music. Be a good sport and watch him play. It is special to him. He wants to share his game with you. Be pleasant and feel honored.

Of course, there is such a thing as overcompromise. There's no need to shop with her *every* time, nor would she want to perspire on the links *every* weekend while trying to swat mosquitoes and pretending to enjoy watching you shoot 128. And, no, it's not necessary to go to lunch or dinner with her parents *every* week. This is where consideration comes back into the picture. You can be considerate and compromise on a dinner now and then, while she could be considerate of you and compromise by trying to space out the dinners.

Marriage, ideally, should be a series of compromises. In reality, most of us just "trade" some things we don't especially like for others we enjoy. For instance, it is nice having someone there at night. It's a treat to have dinner prepared after a hard day and a comfort to have the laundry picked up and towels washed. On the other hand, it's nice to have a man around for protection instead of a Doberman. Everyone finds it satisfying to have someone who appreciates their efforts, because we all like to be appreciated. It's just plain enjoyable to have a companion with whom to share new experiences and a life together. Love and being loved brings a secure feeling, and it is rewarding to watch your love grow into a family, then to pass this love on to your children and hope they will follow suit.

TAKE NOTHING FOR GRANTED

The list of "how not to lose 'em when you get 'em" can go on *ad infinitum*. Trouble is, after a while, we take each other for granted, just *assuming* our partner will do a certain thing at a certain time. You somehow just plan on them being there when you return from aerobics. At a certain time every evening they'll surely come through that door and will take care of the garbage, or discipline the kids, or whatever. Big things, little things, *thousands* of things go on each day in a household we just take for granted. We never worry or even appreciate much of this until it is no longer there.

Communication, consideration, and compromise: three essentials in any relationship. Tenderness isn't so bad in a relationship either. Even when he comes back from taking out the garbage, why not say, "Honey, thanks for taking out that smelly garbage. You don't know how much I appreciate it." With words like that, the sonofagun will be taking out the garbage forever, maybe even for the neighbors. When dinner is over, why *not* walk over, put your arms around her, and give her a kiss. "Thank you, sweetheart. That was a terrific dinner. I love you so much." Yeah, guys and gals, this stuff works. In fact, if you practice, it could become a very desirable habit. Sure, sure, maybe it sounds like work to you — and it *is*! But that is what we call compromise too — a little niceness on your part for the effort on her part, or *vice versa*.

Remember that gifts and surprises are important. I had the best time one day surprising my girlfriend with a "treasure hunt." Beginning with a short note telling her to go to the refrigerator and look on the third shelf, there she found her favorite yogurt. Taped to the package of yogurt was a note leading to the pantry, which disclosed peanut brittle. Another clue led to the piano bench and page 100 in the music book. Then to the china cabinet for a copy of a new book she had wished for. Another note on the back cover of the book sent her to yet another part of the house and, yes, the final clue led her to the bedroom. Think she wasn't *ready*? New foreplay, guys. Try it!

The only time it took was about fifteen minutes to write the notes and prepare hiding places, and just a little longer to do the shopping. I had more fun than she — even enjoyed planning it. Sharing her joy while she went from place to place all happy and giggly was great. That, my friends, is consideration and care. It is also smart. In fact, seems like it's time to do another hunt of that sort. Why not try it with the one you love?

Do buy her a piece of candy or bubble gum, or one of those supermarket bouquets of flowers next time you're in the store. Surprise her with a gift on days other than the "expected" ones. If you have big bucks, buy something nice. If you don't, buy something romantic, not practical. Money or not, try sending balloons, candy, or flowers. It truly is the *thought* that will help a relationship flourish.

CONSTRUCTIVE CRITICISM

Be easy on the criticism. This person who was so perfect a few months ago has, all of a sudden, added some eccentricities here and there, ones of which you were unaware during the beginning of the relationship. Well, it's difficult to know everything about a person in a few weeks or months. You made a list of what you want, and the list of things unacceptable, but somewhere along the line a few of your partner's irritating quirks must have escaped notice.

There are ways to handle these. Suppose he chews with his mouth partially open. "Max, for chrissakes, close your big mouth when chewing!" Is that the way to cajole him out of an obnoxious habit? Hardly, unless you want to cause hard feelings. Why not point out some oaf at a restaurant and say, "Honey, will you look at that guy over there? The one with his mouth open while he's chewing. I can see his food digest." Max might get the picture and become aware of what *he's* doing.

In college, I recall having a date with a girl to go to the beach. When she raised her arm to remove her cover-up, I noticed four or five days' stubble under her arms. Ugh! Who could believe it? How could this pretty, bright, seemingly aware girl not shave, especially when she knew it was a beach date? Veins stuck out in my neck while I was trying to turn my head and not stare. It turned me off. Every time she raised her arms above rib level, I turned my head. On the drive home, during idle and varied conversation, I mentioned to her a story about my brother, who, in World War II, took a razor with him on dates because the European girls rarely shaved their legs or armpits, a custom to which he was not accustomed. A week or so later at a school track meet (the girl was a cheerleader), I made an effort to peek under her arms. She had shaved.

Suppose your wife has a certain dress she likes that you can't stand. Let's suppose she wears it often. Do not say, "Phyllis, if you wear that pink, flowery outfit one more time, I'm going to *vomit* on it." That will hurt her feelings and the evening will have been shot. Instead, ask if you can go to the closet with her and help pick out something to wear for that evening. Married or dating, she'll like the idea. When going through her wardrobe and spotting that pink piece of *crap* you hate so much, just bypass it. If she makes a grab for it, don't karate chop her on the wrist, just brush her aside gently and move on to something else.

Of course, that will only be a momentary victory since the next time, or the next, she will want to wear that pink "thing" again. Then, try this. "Honey, I know there are some shirts of mine that you don't especially like, right? Then I want you to come to my closet and let's weed them out, then call up Goodwill." Trust the fact that she doesn't like some of your shirts. Then maybe you can suggest going through *her* closet too. She probably won't like it when you suggest ditching the pink rag, but will be aware it is not your favorite and will either agree to trash it or wear it when she is not with you. It is worth the effort.

Yes, those wanting romance should be considerate, caring, subtle, and gentle. If you are not naturally romantic, at least "think" romance once in a while. Watch foreign movies — the Italians, the Spanish, and the French. Ah yes, watch the way French men romance their sweethearts and wives (not especially at the same time).

BE AWARE—AND CARE

There are two other virtues rather essential to a successful relationship: *care* and *awareness*. So many of these terms are interrelated that we could go on and on, but bear with me a bit longer because you *would* like your relationship to go on and on, wouldn't you?

You must *care* about that person. If she is lifting something heavy, have concern about her welfare and not whether you have full hospitalization to cover her if she breaks her back. Spoil that lady of yours. And you, madam, don't make him feel like a king — convince him he *is* a king. "Care" is such a small word, yet so very profound. If she has a headache, offer to get an aspirin and some water. If he seems to be worn out from cutting the lawn in that hot sun (even if it's a riding mower), mix up a pitcher of tea or lemonade for him because you *care*.

Now, on to *awareness*. You don't have to be a Rhodes Scholar to know when something is not right with your marriage or love affair. You don't need a diploma showing you graduated *cum laude* to know when you've neglected or disappointed one another far too often. You certainly don't need a

Let's Keep 'Em Once We Get 'Em

degree in philosophy to know that what you're doing is not enough.

Not caring is one thing. When one is not even aware of obvious discontent in a partner, it's probably because the person no longer cares. It's not that they're too stupid to recognize it. Sliding into a *habit* of taking things for granted and feeling certain things will always go along on an even keel is common. If you are oblivious of problems ahead, it's the same as a ship without a compass about to encounter an approaching storm. There most certainly will be movement, but in which direction? You're not "aware" of a problem — until it's too late.

Go off for a few hours and be alone. Get that damned pencil and paper out again and write down the times you *haven't* done things your own common sense tells you *should* have been done. Jot down the times you *didn't* want to do something he or she suggested just because you "didn't feel like it." Remember the words, the BIG "Cs": *communication, consideration,* and *compromise.* Then think of *care* and *awareness.*

If you do care, it's time to show it. If communication has been bad, begin trying. If compromise hasn't been a strong suit, it isn't too late to start. And don't leave out consideration, my favorite word. With consideration we would never be unhappy.

Yes, you've got 'em now. Let's love 'em, spoil 'em, help 'em, appreciate 'em, and keep 'em!

Chapter Fourteen

Pets to Combat Loneliness

Pets aren't only for kids, you know. Owning a pet is a responsibility and an excellent way to spend some "alone" moments. Doctors say one's blood pressure takes a *fifteen-point* dip when a pet sits in their lap and they stroke it softly and gently. Perhaps if you had stroked your mate in the same manner, or they had done it to you, *both* of you would be cuddling the little pet.

When talking "pets," that's an extremely broad category. Most likely the doctor's report meant animals like dogs, cats or rabbits, or maybe even a pony. I'm not certain if a goldfish, boa constrictor, or pet alligator can lower blood pressure, but if you like those types of animals, it is your choice.

When I was a kid, my parents brought home a little puppy of unknown heritage. It was a female. I named her Gal. The dog had long brown ears and long legs, a hound of some type. I loved that dog more than I did my brother. Why not? He tried to *trade* me to a kid down the block for a frog! My little puppy grew and grew and grew. I weighed about fifty pounds, as I recall, and Gal weighed about forty pounds. We went everywhere together, and a few nights I even slept in the shed on her blanket with this big mutt cradled in my arms.

One day after school Gal wasn't there waiting for me, rushing up to almost bowl me over and drag her large, wet tongue across my face. She had been poisoned by a mean neighbor. I went to get my dad's gun off the wall to shoot that lady, but naturally my parents stopped me. My heart was broken. Who could ever forget putting the lifeless form of my brown pal in the wagon and bringing her home to a burial place behind our house? I put flowers and a cross on her grave and went out to visit her every day after coming home from school. A few months later my dad brought another dog home and, in time, I learned to love it too.

This was my first experience with loneliness. Someone I loved very much was taken from me, and my dad, equipped with a fourth-grade education, knew a "new partner" was what would help soothe the wound.

As I write these words, my mind reflects back on those long-ago years Gal and I played, slept, and ate together. Yes, she was the whole world to me.

About three years ago I spotted a little pooch in the pet store . . . priced at $300. I lived in a condo and also traveled a lot. My girlfriend and I liked the dog, but agreed that owning one would be unfair to the dog, and would create problems for us. We drove home and went upstairs in silence. Then we turned to face each other and sprang up. She got her purse and I got my keys. We sped to the pet store but, too late — the dog had been sold! The lucky couple were just leaving the store, the puppy nestled in the woman's arms. Not having the nerve to try and buy it for a higher price, we returned home feeling we had lost something special.

I grabbed the newspaper and checked the want-ad section for pets. A short time later, we were admiring our new little dog: a dachsund. We called him Chase. He is our little son.

He is smart and neat and a wonderful companion. Of course, most dogs of this breed sport names like "Heidi," "Schotzi" or "Weiner" but Chase was named after an acquaintance of ours who is lazy, will eat anything, sleep anywhere, never works, but is fun to have around.

Think about if for a minute and if you do choose a pet, be as careful in choosing one as you would a mate. Well, almost. If the dog is too large, don't buy him for your apartment; they need room to run and play. Cats are good pets. A recent survey tells that nineteen million Americans own cats. Cats are clean, they do not require a daily walk, as do dogs, and they are fairly independent, perfect companionship for busy single individuals who still have a need to nurture a warm animal.

I knew a girl who had a bird (a parakeet or maybe a canary) and she spent an hour or so each day talking to her little feathered friend. During such a one-way conversation, the bird chirped back a few times and she was convinced her pet understood and replied. But *I* didn't understand. When she left the room, I got some of the same sounds when thumping the cage with my finger. The point is, her parakeet was companionship for her and she enjoyed its presence and its antics as much as most people enjoy their friends.

Fish are easy pets to keep. But if you do decide to become involved in fish, I recommend the tropical ones as opposed to goldfish or the saltwater variety. Goldfish all tend to look somewhat alike. Saltwater fish are certainly beautiful, but if you don't maintain the exact temperature prescribed by the fish guidebook, you'll find them floating upside down or maybe with one eye hanging out. Tropical fish are not as expensive as the saltwater type, and they are as colorful and as interesting as any. And unlike goldfish, they don't leave those long lines of black ca-ca all over the bottom of the aquarium. Besides, you can buy some other type of fish that will keep your fish tank clean. Yep, they go along the bottom like little Dustbusters, cleaning and moving. Somehow I can't imagine

Pets to Combat Loneliness 155

a fish becoming a "companion" as a dog or cat would. Burial by flushing them down the toilet tends to prove that point without further discussion.

It's pleasant having an animal in your lap when you're relaxed, reading a book, listening to music, or watching TV. One can spend a pleasant evening at home alone without being totally alone. That "responsibility" I mentioned helps occupy your mind too. Animals must be trained, walked, fed, and taken to the doctor; it's almost like having an infant. And you can use the little boogers. Evenings and weekends, take them to the park and train them to go chase a dog whose owner is appealing to you. Or, have them run into a group of picnickers and maybe "worm" an invitation to join them. Yes, pets are great conversation starters.

My dog, Chase, helps relieve tension and gives me an often-needed distraction to break the monotony. He's my pal, my little guy. Chase needs me and I feel that, many times, I need him too. I smile at many of his antics and laugh at many more.

The kind of pet you decide upon is, of course, an individual thing, the same as the type of food you eat, car you drive, and companion you select. If conditions warrant, I strongly recommend a pet. You'll be doing yourself and the animal a favor. They truly do take up many otherwise lonely moments.

THEY'RE PRACTICALLY CHILDREN

Two of my friends who are in their mid-fifties didn't take the time to have children and haven't regretted it for a moment. But they do have a dog you'd swear was their child. Everywhere they go, the dog comes along. When they fly to the coast, the dog gets packed away and goes with them. On fishing trips, the dog is on deck enjoying the sun. At breakfast, even at a restaurant, the dog gets an order of bacon, eggs, and toast. And he not only anxiously awaits their return to the van with the food, but *expects* it. The dog gets daily vitamins, worm pills, weekly baths, and manicures at the vet. They've tried a sixty-dollar electronic flea collar on him too. The dog is their child.

Another friend owns a cat. She cares for that cat as much as many people care for their children. The cat, Persian, I think, is as bright as most kids. He waits by the door for her to come home from work and sits in a chair when she eats. He sits next to her on the sofa while she reads, then cuddles in her arms the second she puts down the book, as though he knows it's time to "do his thing." And, of course, she talks to the cat and the cat mews back during the appropriate pauses. When there is company over, the cat sits in one corner of the room, seemingly satisfied his mistress has someone over whom she enjoys. Yes, her cat takes up just enough of her time, yet not too much. Why not have a pet that suits your personality and need?

Yet another friend has a horse. Each evening after work, he goes out and brushes his horse, checks with the stable keeper to see that the horse has been fed and watered properly, then he either rides or walks the horse around the arena by the halter. Sometimes, when riding, he allows the horse to wander while he simply enjoys the moment. The horse is more than a pet; it is his friend. He attends horse shows and meets a lot of new people while participating in overnight rides. Spending more time with his animal was an easy alternative to combating lonely moments when he and his girlfriend split up. He is "repairing" nicely and his horse helped keep him busy.

It's wonderful to feel "needed," and most certainly, pets need us. My vote for a pet, if your condition warrants it, is up near the top of my "should have" list to help ease those lonely times. And it isn't necessary to be alone in order to own and enjoy a pet. Many couples, many families, and many people who are not lonely own pets.

We can learn from pets also. We can, perhaps, even train ourselves through these pets to understand tolerance, to show warmth and love, to share mutual feelings — the same feelings necessary to sustain a successful relationship with humans.

I was interviewed on the Morton Downey, Jr. show a year or so back when I was promoting a book. Friends asked why. They reasoned the only people who watched his show think wrestling is real and voted for Wallace in the presidential election a few years back. I went anyway. I reasoned it couldn't hurt. It didn't. But I knew I was asking for trouble.

The first words from Morton Downey's lips were: "Here's a writer from Texas who says treat your wife like a dog!"

"Wrong, Mort," I replied. "I said treat your wife the way I treat my dogs. Hug 'em, love 'em, kiss 'em, pet 'em, pay for their needs and medical expenses, forgive their minor frailties, surprise them with little 'happys,' worry about 'em when you're away, miss 'em and be happy to see 'em when you return. If the majority of the men treated their wives the way I treat my dogs, we'd have a world full of happy women." It's *true,* and I mean no disrespect to womankind in using this parallel.

Chapter Fifteen

What Do Old Folks Do?

Being old and alone is certainly more serious than being young and alone, but it's a fact of life most of us will have to face one of these days. At what age do people become "old folks," since age truly is a state of mind? I've seen "old" people at thirty-five and "young" people at seventy-five. "Old" is an individual thing. Look at a person without taking their chronological years into consideration. If you like 'em, be their friend, enjoy them, love them, or marry them. Whatever makes you happy, why not do it?

I remember being seventeen in the service, and writing to Mom. "They're all pretty old, Mom. Most of the guys are twenty and the old man is twenty-five." I must have been a slow learner, because about five years later, I saw a man working out on the big-bag in a boxing gym. He was hitting the bag frequently and with power.

"You're in pretty good shape," I told him.

"Thanks," he replied between deep breaths. "I like keeping in shape. Got to, ya know. Being thirty means I have to work a little harder than I did while in my twenties."

I didn't say anything, but I thought about how he was really pounding that bag — at thirty, yet! Maybe thirty isn't that old after all.

No matter, it's six of one and half-a-dozen of the other when it comes to being old and lonely. Seems like you have a larger storehouse of good memories to call upon than younger counterparts, as well as interesting stories to relate that tend to hold many younger people in awe. Perhaps you have children and maybe even grandchildren with which to share these winter years.

Let's suppose you are in the "older" category and your mate of so many wonderful years has just passed away. What to do? Well, almost any person with a sense of humor, who is easy to get along with, will be welcome in the homes of children or grandchildren. Most can easily make room for "Grand-pop" and "Grandma" too. Those who have financial means can opt for one of those places in Florida, California, or a health spa in the desert. Those choosing a retirement home should know there are those that are almost like going back to summer camp — only instead of kids there are a majority of septuagenarians.

For those who are curious, "old folks" do the same things as "young" folks. They just take a little longer doing it and maybe don't do it as frequently. Most of the retirement homes have parties, dances, outings, and many other activities. They might have to trade in the monkey for the waltz, or the jitterbug for the two-step, but they make it.

In my interviews with dozens of older folks, several enlightening stories emerged. One of the more delightful interviews was with Lance, a seventy-six-year-old playboy who was living in one of those middle-priced nursing homes. Lance was thoroughly enjoying this place. His usual dress was white pants, blue socks, white sneakers, and a T-shirt. He had no hair, false teeth, and a superb sense of humor, and definitely thought of himself as a lady-killer. This man didn't think of himself as old, or else he didn't act like it. Some of the more shy gentlemen marveled at the way Lance "operated." They liked him, and he kept them smiling with his romantic roguery. Yes, he must have really been a charmer in yesteryear. At the time, this Valentino was "playing the field," dating about a half-dozen of the forty or so ladies in the home. He was always smiling, flirting, and cheering others up. He was their leader. I asked Lance about sex. He was candid with me on the subject. "I date a lot of the girls around here," he mused, "but the one I care for most, the one I am sexually loyal to, is Loretta."

I had a chat with Loretta. She, too, was candid. "He's terrific," she said about Lance. "We are 'alone' about twice a week, maybe one time in my room and another time in his. We have private rooms," she added. "Well, semiprivate. Our roommates know our signals and stay out during 'those times.'" She spoke openly and was not ashamed — not one hint of shame. I was proud of her.

When I talked to Maude, who was seventy-four, she admitted to several hand-holding times and lots of hugging, a little kissing, but no sex. She said she was "waiting for the right man" but, she sighed, "I'm afraid I was married to the right man for over fifty years and nobody else could replace him." She had been widowed only three years and her children thought it was best she be put in a home. She tried living with her kids for three months and was truly lonely. She needed the companionship and camaraderie found only with those in her own age bracket. Here, she was happy and had many friends. She wasn't "looking for that special guy," she added, "but, if he came along, I'd know." I hope she finds him, or at least, doesn't stop looking.

As I walked out the front entrance I saw Lance and Loretta on the porch swing. They waved to me. I've gone back at least once a month for the past two years and attended some of their parties and we exchanged gifts two Christmases. I feel both happy and sad every time I leave. Maybe it's looking into the future, wondering what I'll be doing or where I'll be when reaching that stage in life.

It's difficult for anyone to visualize their own grandmother and grandfather having sex, but it happens! Dr. Reubens says a person can have sex until reaching 120 years of age if they have (1) a proper diet, (2) sufficient exercise, and (3) the right partner. Yes, being old doesn't mean you're dead.

There are still tennis matches to enjoy. You can take vacations, go on a shipboard cruise, and still fall in love. Having fun, having sex, and chasing the opposite sex is not confined only to the young.

Many people cannot fathom their grandparents "making out." But, kids, that's the way it is. In fact, why not hope your widowed or divorced grandparent *does* make out? All ages deserve to go on living, the same as you. There is no reason ever to be lonely regardless of age, if you don't choose to be lonely. Why should it be earth-shattering to you for Grandmom to pursue a man at her age? The world is faster to forgive or excuse the old than it is the young.

So, if your loved one of many years recently passed away, first seek the comfort of your family. You knew it was going to happen sooner or later, so there's been time to think about it and make some plans. Now is the time to follow those plans. Your departed loved one would have wanted it that way.

IT'S TIME TO LIVE AGAIN

Begin to take short walks, then longer ones. Keep your sense of humor, positive attitude, and your spirit up. No, there is no reason to be lonely. You've got experience in life, and now is the time to put it to use. Good luck and may God bless, but you must get off that over-sixty-year-old duff and *do* things. So, you're not rich. Then go to bingo parties; go for walks in the park with friends; visit a local "retirement home" and meet some people. Help others live the remaining years of their lives with your companionship and good sense of being.

Some who have been widowed and are alone may have limited funds and no children or grandchildren to call upon, no relatives with which to seek refuge or solace. Surely there is social security or some retirement. Plan now in order to be able to spend wisely; there is a necessity to be thrifty on your fixed budget. Many years of experience should have taught you to live within your means.

Well, perhaps there's a little town about 100 miles or less from your big city where the cost of living is lower, and the pace is slower. For instance, near my small country place there are about four little cities in one county where senior citizens are a majority. They have state-supported nutrition centers and halls where the older folks meet and have lunch, parties, visit with each other, and make plans. Many of these people are living together because they are accustomed to companionship. Some of these "live-togethers" are of the same sex and some are not. Why not have a buddy to share these autumn years, sort of a reverse in time? Most kids have companions of the same sex, why not seniors?

Here, in the country, one can rent a small farmhouse with a few acres of land for as little as $200 a month. This, split in half, is just a hundred dollars. Some of these folks have chickens and ducks, maybe a cow or two, a garden and some wild game to hunt. They are near lakes where they can fish. Sounds fun to me, like camping out when we were kids.

There's one large house where five people live: three men and two women. They have a wonderful life together. Dinner might come from their garden or from a fishing trip. They have parties, play games, go to church, visit the nearby nutrition center, and share their stories with others the same age. They were marvelous to interview.

George is seventy-seven and appointed head of the family of five. He gathers all the monthly checks and puts them into separate accounts. The others have confidence in his honesty and managerial ability. George was an accountant for over forty years, so he knows how to handle their funds. Thelma and Francine are the ladies of the house. Each person has his own room and they share two refrigerators and three bathrooms. The monthly rent is $600. Utilities vary with the seasons, but mostly in the summer they use ceiling fans. For the winter months they have a large fireplace and two woodburning stoves — one for warming toast and cooking popcorn, the other a potbelly type, for heat. There are individual butane heaters in each bedroom for the cold nights.

The men make short trips to the woods with a wagon and chainsaw to cut branches and small trees. These folks use it wisely, being careful not to "cut out" an area. The youngest in the group is Harvey, who is seventy-two. He exercises every day and just seems to shine when complimented by the others when he brings home the largest pieces of wood.

The main ingredient common with these folks is their ease in getting along with others. A sense of humor and a positive personality are important at any age.

None, apparently, had become "involved," and all were satisfied with the arrangement. Francine has a date now and then with Herb from the nutrition center, and Thelma went away a weekend every two months to visit her daughter in the city. Marvin, the seventy-four-year-old who did most of the hunting and fishing, dated now and then too. Their combined income was over $3,000 a month, and they lived in comfort and security, independent from anyone. I envied them.

YOU'RE NOT ALONE

So you see, being old does not mean life is at an end, even at a standstill. It all depends on what *you* want to make of it. If you're a moody person, a negative person, or a cantankerous old bastard, I guess you will have a hard time of it. Hopefully, age has mellowed the bad moods, foul temper, and the need to be warlike. *Consideration* and *compromise* are words we should try to live by at any age. If you're likable, sweet or fun to be around, interesting or will work with others, you will have little trouble in later years, even with no family or relatives to come to the rescue. There will be no need to be rescued. Just know where to look to find others in the same situation and there are *millions*. Why not "bunk in" with someone else whom you enjoy and share expenses? What about that five-person house? They were enjoying life like young children, each sharing some responsibility, each contributing to make others comfortable. Yes, there's still a wonderful world out there waiting for those who look, a place to enjoy regardless of age.

I have a friend I'll call Mr. Lee, who is in his seventies. He is an artist who lives in a nice home, again in a rural area, and has adequate savings to see him through the remainder of life. "Unless," he smiles, "I make it over 110." Mr. Lee's health is good and he has a quick wit. He lives alone and is content. His wife of forty-two years died about eight years ago and "there was an adjustment," he tells me, "but it took me thirty years to accept the fact that I had to compromise and now, I do as I damned well please."

I asked about his daily routine. "Up at six and read the morning paper. Then whip up a breakfast of eggs, sausage or maybe pancakes. Sometimes I have a bowl of cereal, not unlike most other breakfasts over the past fifty years. Thing is, I can watch the soaps *I* choose, can put my book and glasses down on the kitchen counter without fear of them being put away. I can watch sports *all* day Sunday for the pros, all day Saturday for the colleges and any other damn time I please without hearing a squawk from anybody."

Now and then he comes down to Linda's Country Kitchen for breakfast and we talk about politics, sports, the economy — everything. I see Mr. Lee at the local bank, the library, the grocery store, and sometimes pass his brightly painted bass boat while scouring the lake for the right spot for fishing. He has adjusted well.

"I loved Edna and adjusted my ways to meet hers, as I'm certain," he sighs, "she did for me. I pray for her now and then, talk to her often before going to sleep at night, but I don't want another wife. Naw, it took too long for us to learn about each other and I'm content to visit friends. A son or grandson drops by now and then, and I make about four trips a year for a few days at a time to visit them, usually on holidays. I paint when I feel the urge, and work on about three canvases at the same time. I still sell, ya know, but I paint mostly for enjoyment."

Asked about the nights, the time when people alone feel it the most, he says, "Nights are just like days. I microwave supper and watch TV or read. The food you can microwave now is delicious and even nutritious to a degree. I take my vitamins, walk around the neighborhood for exercise, and do my own laundry. I never wear a suit, so just scrubbed pants and a 'Lee ironed' shirt is all I need. I'm enjoying my life, but in a different way. Certainly there is an adjustment period, but those happen all through life whether you're with someone or not." Mr. Lee, in my opinion, is okay. No need to be concerned over him.

WHEN YOU HAVE TO RELY ON OTHERS...

Poverty and *poor health* seem to be the two most profound misfortunes of old age. If you're in poor health, not many people want you and, if so, not for long. If you're without funds — savings, pension, social security — that too often puts a limit on your welcome. In the vast majority of the cases interviewed, these two factors were the most predominant. It interfered with the lives of the children or grandchildren and made the lives of those being cared for unpleasant. But then, these two factors aren't confined to the plight of the old but to those of any age.

One young couple had both their grandparents living with them. The situation, in this instance, put a damper on their lives. Sure they could leave the three kids with these live-in babysitters, but the grandparents were constantly trying to teach their grandchildren how to rear the kids. "We couldn't watch TV when *we* were kids," they would preach. The answer to that is there probably *wasn't* any TV when they were kids, only radio. "Our parents made us eat all our food. Waste not, want not," they chanted almost in unison when one of the great-grandchildren left food on the plate. And this went on and on. It made life a bit gray for everyone.

If it's imperative to go live with children or grandchildren, make an effort to compromise some habits, if this is at all possible. Make certain to be a help and not a hindrance. *Never* get on an advice-giving routine. You had your chance at your kids. Give them a chance at their kids. Please, grandparents or great-grandparents (and I know I'm asking a lot), be smiling and helpful, and let them make their own mistakes. Chances are you are needed, wanted and loved, but you are wiser now and it's time to show it.

I have another set of "older" friends named Charlie and Doodles. Charlie is a retired truck driver. He and Doodles have been together since their teens. They're really not "old." Remember: age is a state of mind, not a tally of the number of years lived.

Charlie and Doodles have a resale shop. It's a three-room store filled with furniture and knickknacks scattered everywhere in a sort of planned disorder. Both get up at six each morning, read the paper, and enjoy breakfast at their favorite haunt, which is on the way to their business, an eight-mile drive. They cheerfully greet customers and exchange all the latest news. Charlie and Doodles are a team. They socialize, make a living, and boast how well the world is treating them. They are happy, wonderful people, and they are enjoying life.

An excellent "close-to-home" example of grandparents being watched over is that of my wife's grandmother. We call her Gran. She and her husband divorced about ten years ago after being together most of their adult lives, almost forty years. He lived but a few miles from Gran and took a new wife, but still visited Gran once a week because they were friends. I'm certain he still loved Gran and, *heaven knows*, she loved him.

About a year ago, Granddad died. Gran has hidden her grief and her increased loneliness reasonably well. We hope this adjustment period won't be so hard on her since, for the past ten years, she has had to contend with only intermittent visits from her former husband and forever love.

All the children love her, one daughter and two sons. There are grandkids now, about ten of them, and they take turns visiting Gran. It isn't a chore for them, either; rather, something they all look forward to.

Gran is a lovable and interesting person. She maintains her home of over forty years and now lives alone. And she intends to do so for many more years. Her lifestyle hasn't changed much. And even though she spends most of her time alone, she isn't lonely. Gran has a support-system of friends, family, and neighbors to rely upon. But most importantly, she has a cheerful disposition and is at peace with herself.

Many of you "old folks" should take a few moments to reflect on your present situation. Perhaps with only a few minor adjustments, you, too, could find more contentment and enjoyment for the remainder of the "golden years." There *is* a good life at seventy, eighty, and even ninety or more. If you're with the one you love, there is no reason to be lonely. If you're not, follow some of the advice in this chapter. Many of these folks were alone, but they found ways *not* to be lonely.

Want to know how *not* to ever be lonely?

(1) Have a POSITIVE ATTITUDE
(2) Keep a good SENSE OF HUMOR
(3) STAY BUSY, and...
(4) Have FRIENDS

Do these things and you have most of it conquered.

A Final Note

I hope those of you who have reached this point in my book have enjoyed it and learned a lot. Most of what I've shared with you came from people much like yourselves. I also hope that my candor and some of the "brutal reality" hasn't offended anyone. I mean to be your best friend and tell you the truth.

Some may think that *How Not To Be Lonely Tonight* is written in a manner to tell you how to go out and find a companion for the evening. There certainly are tips that will do that. But overall, I want people to be happy with *themselves* as well as with a relationship. The advice offered throughout the book will give you what you need for long-term happiness — not just tonight.

Some others may wonder how this book could help a gay individual. *How Not To Be Lonely Tonight* is for everyone, regardless of sex *or* sexual preference. All of the rules can be followed by a gay person too, though there may be slight changes in perspective here and there.

It is true that my book is written for anyone regardless of sex; however, oddly enough, women read this book on a ratio of about nine to one over men. It is a book that men *should* read, though, to gain greater understanding. So women, buy a copy for your man. Show it to a relative or friend. (But don't *lend* it; surveys show that only one in twenty are returned!)

I realize it's impossible to be happy all of the time. But do your best to try. Remind yourself when you reread different passages of the book that if you have a positive attitude, fun sense of humor, stay busy, and enjoy friends, the odds are good that you'll not be lonely tonight — or ever!